# A Beginner's Guide to the Study of Religion

## Second Edition

## Also available from Bloomsbury

*The Daoist Tradition*, Louis Komjathy

*Religion, Postcolonialism and Globalization*, Jennifer Reid

*Religions and Environments: A Reader in Religion, Nature and Ecology*, edited by Richard Bohannon

*The Study of Religion,* 2nd edition, George D. Chryssides and Ron Geaves

# A Beginner's Guide to the Study of Religion

Second Edition
Bradley L. Herling

**Bloomsbury Academic**
An imprint of Bloomsbury Publishing Plc

B L O O M S B U R Y
LONDON · OXFORD · NEW YORK · NEW DELHI · SYDNEY

**Bloomsbury Academic**
An imprint of Bloomsbury Publishing Plc

50 Bedford Square
London
WC1B 3DP
UK

1385 Broadway
New York
NY 10018
USA

www.bloomsbury.com

**BLOOMSBURY and the Diana logo are trademarks of Bloomsbury Publishing Plc**

First edition published 2007

This second edition published in 2016
Reprinted 2016 (four times)

**British Library Cataloguing-in-Publication Data**
A catalogue record for this book is available from the British Library.

ISBN: HB: 978-1-4725-0692-4
PB: 978-1-4725-1277-2
ePDF: 978-1-4725-0521-7
ePub: 978-1-4725-0603-0

**Library of Congress Cataloging-in-Publication Data**
A catalog record for this book is available from the Library of Congress.

Typeset by Newgen Knowledge Works (P) Ltd., Chennai, India
Printed and bound in the United States of America

# Contents

# Preface for Students and Teachers

## Beginnings

My own involvement with the academic study of religion goes back to sophomore year in college. I had not yet declared a major and one night ducked into a lecture by Fredric Jameson, on the spur of the moment. At the time I had no idea that Jameson was a prominent American intellectual, and his presentation painted a rather dreary picture of the possibility of positive social and political change. But the discussion after the lecture led to something of an epiphany. One of my friends bravely stood up and asked a question that went something like this: "Professor Jameson, you seem to be saying that even people who are really out there artistically are still just sell-outs. So if genuinely creative people can't change anything, then what about the rest of us? What are we supposed to do if we want to change the world?"

Jameson paused for a moment and said, "Know everything." And that's pretty much where he left his answer.

Since then I have learned how to fit that answer into the broader context of Jameson's thought. But when I first heard it, this response posed a challenge that only an ambitious but somewhat naïve undergrad could take literally. That semester I was taking my first classes in the academic study of religion, and something clicked. Religion seemed to be everywhere, so maybe studying it was the best way to "know everything." Soon after hearing this lecture, I decided to become a major in Religious Studies.

I have gotten over the hubris that was originally inspired by Jameson's proclamation, but my teachers and training in the field have consistently reinforced the general idea. The study of religion spans the breadth of human experience and the full range of cultures, from ancient times to our present day. It is an exploration of some of the most powerful ways human beings discover *meaning*, *significance*, and *depth*, as Jonathan Z. Smith has written (and please pardon his lack of gender neutrality):

> What we study when we study religion is one mode of constructing worlds of meaning, worlds within which men find themselves and in which they choose to dwell. What we study is the passion and drama of man discovering the truth of what it is to be human. History is the framework within whose perimeter those human expressions, activities and intentionalities that we call "religious" occur. Religion is the quest, within the bounds of the human, historical condition, for the power to manipulate and negotiate one's "situation" so as to have "space" in which to meaningfully dwell. It is the power to relate one's domain to the plurality of environmental and social spheres in such a way as to guarantee the conviction that one's existence "matters." Religion is a distinctive mode of human creativity, a creativity which both discovers limits and creates limits for humane existence. What we study when we study religion is the variety of attempts to map, construct and inhabit such positions of power through the use of myths, rituals and experiences of transformation.[1]

*Meaning*, *history*, *power*, and *creativity*: religion is at a unique intersection of these elements, taking shape in lived reality. As such, it can be identified within most, if not all aspects of human endeavor, and to that extent, I had the right idea as an undergraduate in my own naïve way, because exploring religion offers the opportunity to follow our curiosity in many directions. It is in this spirit, extending back to my own naïve beginnings in the field, that I have written this book.

## Literacy: Religious and Theoretical

Everyone should be hungry for information about religion these days, and the information is out there, on shelf after shelf at the local bookstore, and in college and university courses. In our complicated world, becoming *literate* is a great reason to study this subject. In his 2007 book, *Religious Literacy: What Every American Needs to Know—And Doesn't*, Stephen Prothero shows that education in religion, and thus knowledge about it, has deteriorated in recent decades. It has gotten to the point that even the devout do not know basic facts about their own traditions. Many Christians, for example, have a tough time naming the four canonical gospels, and about 10 percent of American adults think that Noah's wife was Joan of Arc. Everyone needs to be literate about religion in our day and age, Prothero argues, because it plays such a major role in global affairs, national politics, and everyday life.[2]

This argument is compelling, but we can add to Prothero's plea: learning *how* to look at religion—becoming *theoretically* literate—is just as important as knowing *facts* about it. It is one thing to know the *content* of any given tradition—its beliefs, practices, history, and so on (and Prothero himself has provided an effective survey of the world's major religions in his more recent book, *God Is Not One: The Eight Rival Religions That Run the World*). But what should we do with this data? How should we explain it? What does it mean? What does it mean for us now, especially if we are hungry not only for information, but also for deeper insights?

Indeed, data only means something within a frame of reference, and everyone has his or her own "baggage" when it comes to religion. But most observers are not sufficiently aware of their own standpoint; they take their beliefs, opinions, and perspective to be solid and self-evident. For this reason, among others, we need to focus as much on the *how* as the *what*. Attending to theory and method raises our consciousness about preconceived notions, and as the inquiry proceeds, precise application of key concepts and practices in the study of religion leads to refined, accurate interpretations—in place of isolated opinions and unreflective judgments.

As any teacher in religious studies will attest, introducing this layer of inquiry is not an easy task. Students often find it abstract or uncomfortable, and the agenda for introductory survey courses in religion is often already crowded, so there's just not enough time for anything "meta." Even in courses designed to introduce the academic study of religion as an approach, getting a handle on complex ideas in primary sources can be an imposing challenge. As a response, this book is designed to make theoretical and methodological foundations in the academic study of religion more accessible, and to do so in concise form, as a starting point for further inquiry.

The first step, taken in Chapter 1, is to establish the significance of studying this subject now, in our day and age. The things that we call "religious" are happening all around us, every day, and they inevitably mean something to each of us, as individuals who are wrapped up in them ourselves, or simply because we wish to be informed. Because of the importance of apprehending our own position as students of religion, this first chapter also introduces some basic methodological steps: *self-*

*consciousness*, *comparison*, *defamiliarization*, and *empathy*. Chapter 2 outlines fundamental operations that we associate with taking a *theoretically informed* approach to any given subject. As we undertake the task of *interpreting* and *understanding* religion, we concern ourselves with *definition*, *description*, *explanation*, and *prediction*. With the right admixture of these activities, we have a better shot at bridging the divide between the world of the religious insider and the work of the academic observer. We interpret more effectively and arrive at a better understanding of the subject matter at hand.

In religious studies, this process is built on classic "theoretical ideas" that have been important in shaping the field. Chapters 3 and 4 contain a survey of some of the most significant of these ideas, and each chapter is organized along a distinct axis. Chapter 3 charts a range of theories about the *fundamental experience of religion*, from the *individual* to the *social*, and it contains accounts of Rudolf Otto, William James, Émile Durkheim, Max Weber, Victor Turner, and Clifford Geertz. Chapter 4 describes the theories of Karl Marx, Sigmund Freud, Carl Jung, Mircea Eliade, Ninian Smart, Paul Tillich, and Wilfred Cantwell Smith. Here the theories range from *critique* to *affirmation* of a religious essence. Chapter 5 highlights trends in the contemporary study of religion, which brings the survey of classic theories up to date and documents the rich diversity of voices and approaches that now populate the field. By way of conclusion, Chapter 6 offers some closing reflections on the challenges associated with talking about religion, and also with talking about studying it. This final chapter offers something of a "field guide," a practical summary of the most common questions that students of religion often hear—along with some worthy responses.

This structure essentially mirrors that of the first edition of the book, which was published in 2007, but the content has been updated throughout in this new edition to take account of both recent events and the most up-to-date scholarship in the field, and to reflect feedback on the first edition from students and colleagues. In particular, Chapter 5 on contemporary trends in the field has been significantly enhanced, with more extensive attention to questions of gender, sexuality, race, globalization, secularization, violence, and media in relation to the study of religion. The final chapter is new to this edition, and it represents a kind of homage to many conversations I have had with undergraduates who decide to major in religion—and then need to explain that decision to others. It should also be noted that this second edition of the book links to a Companion

Website at www.bloomsbury.com/a-beginners-guide-to-the-study-of-religion-9781472512772, which contains resources for both students and instructors.

Of course in a short book like this, which is designed primarily to accompany the already busy agenda of a college or university course, the contents are selective, and much has been left aside. And yet I am confident that having worked with this guide, a beginning student (or general reader), will be better prepared for examining the "real stuff," the complex data that we encounter when we study religion. So in my account, I have aimed for conciseness and clarity, hopefully without sacrificing comprehensiveness or complexity. The main goal is to have students *do* something with theory. This means that I often boil the ideas down to encourage application. Each discussion of a major theorist in the field, for example, is accompanied by a section titled "What to look for," which briefly summarizes the main directives of any given approach.

While this book does engage some of the complicated debates that concern scholars, I have emphasized comprehension of the foundations of these debates, rather than their intricate details. This leaves many issues open, issues that instructors and students will hopefully work on together, aided by the Companion Website. To add to this dialogue, I have often included quotations from the primary sources, which supplement the text, provide the basis for further discussion, and invite students to engage these sources in more depth. Toward that end, this book also includes a list of additional readings to keep the student (or the ambitious autodidact) headed in the right direction.

One final note. While this text was primarily written for university and college students enrolled in religion courses, I hope that it will hold interest for "students" of religion in the broad sense: it should provide food for thought for anyone who wants to look into this complex, pervasive phenomenon. It also represents a small but hopefully meaningful contribution to current discussions about the purpose of religious studies among my academic colleagues. For the sake of our students, our departments, our discipline, and for the sake of our world the way it is today, I would argue that the academy needs to see religious studies as more than an administrative title. We should consider allowing that there are in fact very real data for the study of religion today. And we might note that the construction of religion by scholars is largely our (the scholars') obsession; whatever it is that the term "religion" actually references is the world's. As informed observers for whom this branch of research has obviously meant *something*, we should occupy our position as educators, emphasize the promotion of religious literacy and cross-cultural understanding—and thereby get on the side of our fellow global citizens, who so want (or need) to know more.

In the pages of this book, I express these sentiments as much to myself as I do to anyone else.

# Acknowledgments

In the spirit of beginnings, I must recall those who first introduced me to the study of religion at Wesleyan University, those who unknowingly abetted my quest to "know everything": Ron Cameron, Stephen Crites, Gene Klaaren, James Stone, Jan Willis, and Jeremy Zwelling. I also want to extend my gratitude to the mentors at Boston University who assisted me in making the transition from student to teacher—and from youthful expectations to more sustainable ones: John Clayton, Paula Fredriksen, Ray Hart, Robert Neville, and Alan Olson. David Eckel deserves special mention and thanks. His "toolbox" for the study of religion served as an inspiration for this book, as did his elegant approach to teaching in the field.

This book had its origins in the text that I produced for a website sponsored by the American Academy of Religion (AAR) titled "Why Study Religion." For their guidance in getting that project off the ground (and therefore this one as well), I wish to acknowledge both Warren Frisina and Carey Gifford. For giving me the continuing opportunity to work with and present these ideas, I thank Continuum (and now Bloomsbury), and particularly the editor of the first edition of this book, Rebecca Vaughan-Williams, for her encouragement. I must also recognize a set of colleagues who took the time to offer comments on this project in its early stages: Kristi Swenson, Elijah Siegler, Kelly Pemberton, Patricia Lennon, Corinne Dempsey, Tim Vivian, David Frankfurter, and Richard Pilgrim. Thanks also to Martyn Oliver and Shawn Gorman for their valuable feedback on the original text along the way, and a special "shout out" to Gene Gallagher for coming through in a pinch with a fantastic set of responses to the manuscript of the first edition. I would also like to express my appreciation to colleagues in the field who decided to adopt the first version of the book for their classes.

The second edition of the book benefited from further outside commentary and constructive criticism. Lalle Pursglove at Bloomsbury initiated this new edition and provided valuable guidance as I considered modifications. Dhara Patel and Anna MacDiarmid were also very helpful as the text was reconstituted and revised. Colleagues once again provided extremely useful suggestions, and I thank them for their efforts: Davina Lopez, Kathryn Blanchard, and three anonymous reviewers. I am also indebted to my students and colleagues at Marymount Manhattan College, who have contributed to my understanding of the field in innumerable ways. Special thanks to Monica Wiles and Maura Grady, students who offered valuable feedback on the text, and to Maura (again) and Nina Carter, who both rendered assistance in revising the Additional Readings section.

Of course, any flaws or failings in the final product should be attributed to me alone.

Finally, I also wish to thank my wife, Maria, for her encouragement and support, and my daughter, Grace, just for being her.

The invitation to write the copy for the "Why Study Religion" website, which laid the groundwork for this book, came to me from Barbara DeConcini, the former executive director of the AAR, and it represented yet one more door that Barbara opened for me intellectually and professionally. One of the most pivotal chapters in my own experience working with the field occurred during my time as the administrative assistant for the AAR from 1992 to 1994. I often say that I got my Master's in the study of religion from the AAR — and Barbara was my advisor. She has been an unflagging supporter and insightful mentor, and this book certainly would never have been written without her influence.

I would like to dedicate this text to Barbara DeConcini, in recognition of her stewardship of the field over the fifteen years she served as executive director of the AAR, and, personally, out of heartfelt gratitude for her friendship over the years.

## Notes

1. Jonathan Z. Smith, "Map Is Not Territory," in *Map Is Not Territory: Studies in the History of Religions* (Chicago and London: University of Chicago Press, 1993), 290–91.
2. You are invited to take Prothero's religious literacy quiz: http://www.deseret-news.com/article/660205799/Stephen-Protheros-religious-literacy-quiz.html?pg=all.

# 1 Beginnings in the Study of Religion

Over the last two hundred years, predictions that religion would soon disappear have been all too common. In the nineteenth century, for example, philosopher Friedrich Nietzsche declared God dead—and even proposed that we ourselves had killed him. Soon thereafter sociologists began to announce the inevitability of secularization, the process by which religion loses its influence over society and individuals. And later, Sigmund Freud argued that religious belief was a collective illusion that humanity would soon outgrow. Today, scientists claim to be on the verge of "breaking the spell" by showing that religious consciousness evolved as a survival technique that is no longer necessary, and proponents of New Atheism write books that rise to the top of the best-sellers list. So we have to ask: is religion on the way out, and, if so, why should we continue to study it?

When we look at the big picture, it seems that rumors of religion's demise have been seriously exaggerated. For now (and for the foreseeable future) it is here to stay, perhaps because it is more complicated than its critics have suspected. For good or ill, that which we call religion continues to be intertwined with our lives. We find it at the center of global issues and political debates. It appears in art, television, film, and popular music. It surrounds us in our cities, towns, and neighborhoods. It is discovered in the lives of the people we know and love, and (for many of us) within ourselves, as we live out our own beliefs and customs. Despite those who have predicted and at times hoped for its disappearance, this strange, familiar thing keeps showing up, calling out for examination, not as something that is dead or dying, but as a thriving reality—something that, at the very least, we must live with.

If you are reading this book, then you are probably somehow drawn to this reality and want to know more about it. Perhaps you are studying it in a class, or maybe you are exploring it on your own. In either case, before delving into the topic, it is necessary to think about your starting point. *Why is it important to study religion right now? What do you already know about it? What should be your approach?*

This opening chapter will invite reflection on these questions, and along the way you will take some basic methodological steps that will start to bring the subject matter into focus.

## SKEPTICISM ABOUT RELIGION

"Whither is God? . . . I will tell you. *We have killed him*—you and I. All of us are his murderers. But how did we do this? . . . Gods, too, decompose. God is dead. God remains dead. And we have killed him."[1]

Friedrich Nietzsche

"In short not only is the sphere of religion not increasing . . . but it is continually diminishing. This regression did not begin at any precise moment in history, but one can follow the phases of its development from the very origins of social evolution."[2]

Émile Durkheim

"Religion would thus be the universal obsessional neurosis of humanity . . . If this view is right, it is to be supposed that a turning-away from religion is bound to occur with the fatal inevitability of a process of growth, and that we find ourselves at this very juncture."[3]

Sigmund Freud

## Imagining the Reality of Religion

When asked about why they are taking a religion class, students say many different things. Here are some of them:

- "It fulfils a requirement and fits in my schedule."
- "I am Christian/Jewish/Hindu/Muslim/etc. and want to know more about my tradition."
- "I'm interested in different cultures and peoples, and studying religion is a good way to learn about that."
- "I want to know how people live."

What is your answer?

In contemplating your own interest in this subject, take another step and allow your imagination to range. *What do you already know about religion? What examples do you associate with this term? Where does it seem to be happening right now in our world, as you read these words?* Identify your own examples, and then consider these.

If it's the right time of the year, along one of the dusty highways of northern India, a young man wearing an orange t-shirt and matching gym shorts is lying down for a rest in a tent. His shirt features an iron-on image of Shiva, one of the most revered gods in the Hindu tradition. The young man has been walking for five straight days in the blistering heat; he has been sleeping in makeshift camps erected by the side of the road. Why is he doing this? He glances over at the object next to him: an elaborately festooned three-foot long pole (called a *kanwar*) with two jugs of water hanging from either end, suspended above the ground by a pair of sawhorses. He has been shouldering this burden for over a hundred miles, always keeping it off the ground, and now he is halfway home to his village in the Indian countryside. There he made a vow to his god, his family, and his community months ago: to go to the holy Ganges river (Shiva's river) and retrieve its water for the purification of the village shrine. The young man believes that this deed will bring him favor in this life and good karma in preparation for the lifetimes to come.

Meanwhile, on a beautiful Greek island in the middle of the Aegean, a young woman is contemplating the task she has set for herself. At the top of a steep hill, about half-mile away, a large church that houses a miraculous icon beckons to her. She thinks about her younger brother dying of cancer in a hospital in Athens and prepares to crawl up to the church on the cobblestones as thousands have done before. She opts not to wear kneepads, like others have done, nor does she wrap her knees to keep them from bleeding. No, she will crawl with her knees bare, because if she can sacrifice herself and show her devotion to Christ, who himself died to release humanity from its pain and sin, he will intercede on behalf of her brother. And he will be saved.

Now, in some major American city, all the preparations are in place: the DJ, the food, the decorations. It will be a great party. All the relatives are in town, and everyone is having a good time, except for one 12-year-old girl. She is nervous because she just knows that she will "totally mess up" her Torah portion, the passage from the Bible that she has to read in front of everyone at her Bat Mitzvah—or, as her rabbi told her, when she *becomes* a Bat Mitzvah (a daughter of the commandments). She has been practicing intensively, and the rabbi has been very nice, teaching her about why the ritual is so important to being Jewish and giving her his ideas about God's mysterious but persistent care for his people. Despite all that, she is still really nervous—though trying not to show it.

At the same time, a middle-aged man arrives in a European airport as he travels on business from Pakistan. He is neatly but casually dressed in slacks and a button-down shirt, and he keeps his briefcase close at hand. His arrival is a little late, and now he is in a rush because the alarm on his watch is going off. This watch is special: not only does it tell the time, but it also reminds the Muslim wearer when to pray and what direction to face when doing so. The man hurries to the nearest bathroom and washes his hands and face quickly, though he is not able to do the full purification ritual. Then he rushes to the ecumenical chapel, where he arrives just in time. It is time to kneel down, to submit to Allah, as he does (or tries to do) five times a day. Now he reaches into his briefcase and pulls out a small bag containing a folded, plastic prayer mat. He consults his watch, faces Mecca (somewhere off to the southeast), kneels down on the mat, and begins the prayer cycle, which according to Muslim law, he is allowed to condense, because he is in transit. Sometimes travelers must make do, and Allah understands that in his infinite wisdom and mercy.

Moving to a second floor studio in one of the bustling neighborhoods of a Japanese city, people from all walks of life are sitting in a circle, all of them cross-legged, some in full lotus position. Apart from the occasional noise from the street below, the room is very, very quiet because the people are just sitting, just breathing. Their minds are full of thoughts that race back and forth, but, as the Buddha taught, they allow a thought to happen, say to themselves, "That's just a thought!," and then gently try to bring their focus back to just breathing, just sitting. They do not fill their minds with a god, with a saint, or with a feeling. In fact, they want to empty themselves, because the Buddha taught that release from suffering comes from realizing that there is no self.

And now (if it is the right time of year), we check in on a professional baseball game in the United States, at Boston's Fenway Park. During the seventh inning stretch, the crowd sings "God Bless America." In the top of the seventh, one of the best players on the visiting team made the last out, despite having done everything according to his routine, a long and elaborate set of hand gestures and adjustments of batting gloves that get him ready to hit before every pitch. To some observers, they look like a ritual, some kind of obsessive or magical incantation. But he failed to get a hit. Now, in the bottom of the inning, the slugger for the home team approaches the plate. He has no intricate prehitting procedure. He just waits for the pitch he wants, swings mightily, and sends the ball into the Monster seats. But as he crosses home plate, he points to the sky, looks up, and says, "For you." The crowd roars.

In some other part of the world, or maybe not so far away, another one of our fellow human beings is filled with hatred and contempt. He says to himself, "An attack on the faithless would please God. And he who wages this war earns a place of honor in the afterlife." True religion for this devotee is a religion of the original word—and of anger and vengeance. "So much has been done to stamp us out and deny the truth," he mutters, contemplating the messages that his teacher has conveyed to him and his small group of confederates, "but real warriors continue to stand up, fight, and sacrifice themselves for the greater good." It is difficult to pinpoint the location of this imagined but all-too-real portrait—because such voices exist in many places, within many traditions and communities.

We could go like this for a long time; you probably have many of your own stories to add. But let us return to the key point: by considering even this limited set of examples, and by producing your own, you are beginning to contemplate that initial question: *why should I study religion now?*

By way of answer, we have already proposed that religion is not just a vague abstraction. The term seems to refer to an active preoccupation and meaningful set of activities in the day-to-day existence of many of our fellow human beings. This should be reason enough to examine it and take it seriously. What makes people tick? What is important to them? How do they make their choices? How do they live? What gives their lives structure, form, and purpose? In so many cases, it is impossible to answer these questions without understanding religion.

## Religion on the Global Scene

Because it is ingrained in the ways that so many people live, religion proves to be a major factor in the most pressing issues of our day. Whatever else it might be, this wide-reaching phenomenon is *intertwined* with other areas of human concern, including politics, international relations, economics, the environment, and the production of culture. *Where does religion show up on the contemporary global and national scene?* Think about your own examples, and then consider the following points.

> "[I]f I went back to college today, I think I would probably major in comparative religion, because that's how integrated it is in everything we are working on and deciding and thinking about in life today."[5]
>
> John Kerry, US Secretary of State

Religious identification has been receding in a number of European nations for some time, and it is possible that the same trend is emerging in the United States. But these developments should be put in global context. A recent WIN-Gallup International study, for example, found that 59 percent of global respondents identified themselves as religious people.[6] A total of thirty-four nations out of the fifty-seven nations included in the poll had percentages higher than this average. Even more dramatically, the Pew Research Religion & Public Life Project estimated in 2012 that 84 percent of people worldwide are "religiously affiliated," 5.8 billion adults and children out of a world population of 6.9 billion.[7]

Why should we study religion? These figures remind us that in our interconnected, mobile, globalized situation it has become increasingly more likely that we will come into meaningful contact with people from a wide variety of backgrounds—and thus we are also liable to have encounters with a diversity of religious beliefs and practices. For this reason alone, it is wise to be informed. The study of religion will not tell you *everything* there is to know about your fellow global citizens, but it gives you a good starting point, the basis for asking the right questions, and local knowledge that might even help you avoid awkwardness, embarrassment, or even offense. So this is in some sense a practical matter: studying religion is useful interpersonally and even professionally, because in our lives and jobs, a global sensibility—and thus religious literacy—is an increasingly important prerequisite.

In the bigger picture, the issues that face us as global citizens transcend our individual career paths or circles of friends and contacts. When considering the state of environment and nature; conceptions of gender, sexuality, and family; the power of media as a purveyor of culture; the imposition of taxes, government spending, and the nature of economic activity; frameworks of political leadership, citizenship, and nationhood; and the emergence of conflict and violence—when considering all these issues in their global context, religion is a big part of the story.

As an example, let us focus on the last item in the list above: *political struggle, international conflict, and violence.* The beliefs and motivations associated with religion have a remarkable capacity to fuel action, and thus it is a potent ingredient when added to political struggle and social strife.

Religiously inspired terrorism is an obvious and pressing case in point. A recent Pew Research poll found that in 2012, religion-related terrorist activity occurred in 20 percent of the world's nations, and these numbers have been on the rise.[8] Over the last two decades, for example, Muslim jihadists—for example, al-Qaeda and its affiliated groups, Boko Haram, The Islamic State of Iraq and Syria (ISIS), and individuals inspired by these broader movements—have proclaimed war against "the West," causing horrible damage across the globe, in Yemen, Saudi Arabia, Kenya, Tanzania, Nigeria, Indonesia, Turkey, Madrid, London, Paris, Boston, Washington, DC, and, of course, New York City—all in the name of political causes justified by a certain version of Islam.

This phenomenon urgently calls out for understanding—but not all theories are created equal. In the wake of 9/11, for example, the United States and some of its allies declared a global "war on terror," which at times had its own religious overtones: some of its rhetoric suggested that this was a broader war between "the West" and "Islam," a "clash of civilizations." In other words, for some, the "war on terror" became a new crusade.

"We are facing a mood and a movement far transcending the level of issues and policies and the governments that pursue them. This is no less than a clash of civilizations—the perhaps irrational but surely historic reaction of an ancient rival [Islam] against our Judeo-Christian heritage, our secular present, and the worldwide expansion of both."[9]

Bernard Lewis

"We are at war with Islam . . . It is not merely that we are at war with an otherwise peaceful religion that has been "hijacked" by extremists. We are at war with precisely the vision of life that is prescribed to all Muslims in the Koran, and further elaborated in the literature of the hadith, which recounts the sayings and actions of the Prophet."[10]

Sam Harris

However, according to Pew Research polling in 2005, even in the wake of 9/11 most Americans did not perceive the situation this way: only 29 percent responded that the struggle against terrorism represents a fight against Islam as a whole.[11] After 9/11, some were tempted to blame all Muslims for the attacks, but another reaction was to become better acquainted with their tradition. Copies of the Qur'an flew off the shelves, books on Islam became bestsellers, scholars were in intense demand by the media, and undergraduate classes on the topic swelled with interested students. Learning more paid dividends, according to the 2005 poll: the more informed the respondents were, the less inclined they were to think in black and white terms. Instead, the most informed respondents were much more likely to identify Muslim terrorists as "a small, radical group"—not as representatives of the tradition as a whole. This connection between education and a more nuanced perspective was confirmed when Pew Research conducted a similar poll in 2009.[12]

These findings reassert the urgency of studying religion now, in connection with pressing international issues. As people learned more, they discovered that Islam is not al-Qaeda, that the tradition as a whole is complex but not bent on murderous violence, that Muslims themselves most often repudiate terrorist actions (which polls also confirm). We might say that these are positive steps. And yet we can also not deny that some version of Islam has indeed provided a backdrop and inspiration for these actions; that is also something that we need to examine and understand.

It should be made clear that Islamic terrorism is hardly the only form of political violence perpetrated in the name of religion; no tradition has a monopoly on it. For example, in his indispensable book, *Terror in the Mind of God*, Mark Juergensmeyer reinforces this point by discussing not only Islamic terrorism, but also abortion clinic bombings and assassinations in the United States, the struggle between Protestants and Catholics in Northern Ireland, the varieties of religious violence in Israel and Palestine, and attacks perpetrated by Sikhs, Hindus, and Buddhists in Asia.[13] Juergensmeyer and other scholars have driven home the message: to diagnose the nature of conflict on the international stage, we have to know what's at stake for the combatants on all sides, and often this effort requires examination of religious factors (overarching worldview, concepts of the afterlife, mythic and doctrinal conceptions of violence, and so on). To comprehend these factors, we need to engage in analysis that is both methodical and theoretically informed.

For example, while terrorism is often a dramatic product of the interplay between religion, politics, and violence, its backdrop can take many different forms:[14]

- On some occasions religious factions attempt to take over a nation, causing conflict with those who are more secular-minded. This takeover happened in Iran in the revolution of 1979, and in its wake, the pro-West secularists were killed or exiled, along with the members of non-dominant religious minorities. In the wake of 9/11, the "war on terror," and the Arab Spring of 2012, many observers have suggested that a number of nations hang in a similar balance, including Pakistan and Egypt.
- In other situations, the nation is not taken over entirely by a religiously inspired party, but a majority faction sets the terms of culture and politics. Internal strife with rival groups is sometimes the result. In theory, India is not a religious state, for example, and it is a pluralistic democracy. Yet Hinduism is the dominant and most influential tradition there, which has often led to tensions with the most significant minority religious group: Muslims.

- Another type of conflict involves the split of a nation into rival religious factions that possess their own territory and end up fighting a civil war with each other. For years Protestants and Catholics fought this kind of battle in Northern Ireland, such a conflict persists in Sri Lanka where Hindus and (surprisingly enough) Buddhists square off against each other, and of course religion has always played an important role in the strife between Israel and Palestine.
- Finally, we are familiar with situations where the "nation" as a unified entity totally falls apart along religious lines. In these cases, there is no unified nation to be fought over any more; the country effectively dissolves because of sectarian conflict and ends up in fragments. This happened in the former Yugoslavia, where religion played an important role in the creation of the battle-lines; Syria and Iraq are currently in danger of undergoing this kind of disintegration as they face the threat of the movement known as ISIS.

Overall, these types of conflict, which have often created the environment for terrorism to emerge, raise important questions: When and how do cultural and political conflicts take on a religious character? What has happened within various traditions that has radicalized some of their members to such an extent that they commit violence? Is there an inherent connection between religion and violence?

Furthermore, we must note that the persistent, perhaps obsessive attention to religion's role in war, violence, and conflict overshadows other important questions: Can religion be a force for good on the international scene, or does it always end up promoting tension and division? Under what circumstances does religion become an antidote to violence? We should not forget the other side of the coin: religious commitments provided a foundation for movements led by Gandhi in India, Martin Luther King in the United States, the now-exiled Dalai Lama, and Aung San Suu Kyi, the 1991 Nobel Peace Prize winner who defied the oppressive military regime in Burma.

None of this is without complexity and controversy, but the overarching point should be clear: when we consider the most pressing issues that concern us as global citizens, most often religion is part of the equation, sometimes a big part. Therefore, if we wish to understand these issues and address them effectively, religious literacy is necessary, along with careful analysis of the way that religious beliefs, motivations, and practices are intertwined with other major areas of human activity.

# Religion on the National Scene in the United States

Every country has its own unique history with religion. The United States is no exception. You may be familiar with the part of First Amendment of the US Constitution that proclaims, "Congress shall make no law respecting an establishment of religion, or prohibiting the free exercise thereof." This dictate, called the "Establishment Clause," expresses commitments that many Americans hold dear. For one thing, it prevents government from affirming any particular tradition, thereby constructing a barrier against the establishment of a religious state or official national religion. The First Amendment also prevents government from interfering with the "free exercise" of religion and therefore allows it to thrive on the ground. In 2007, the Pew Research Religion & Public Life Project showed that 92 percent of Americans believe in God, for example, and for 56 percent of them, religion is "very important in their lives."[15] More recent polling has suggested some declines in these numbers,[16] and yet faith remains a powerful force in the lives of a significant majority of US citizens.

This has much to do with the deep connection between the history of the American nation and Christianity. But the United States has always been a nation of immigrants, and In recent years, the traditions found in pluralistic, multicultural America have become more prominent than ever. In order for Americans to understand themselves in this historical moment, to contend with their heritage and emerging trends, studying religion must be a priority.

"Just as free speech and a free press distinctively shape and define American politics, society, and culture, so too does freedom of religion. By naming religion and marking it off for special consideration, the Constitution embeds the notion of religion in American culture. Because of the First Amendment, religion is a native category for Americans, a basic, culturally significant classification that we routinely and intuitively use to make sense of the world and explain what is happening to us. That there is religion and that religion matters are axioms of American life."[17]

William Scott Green

This point is particularly vivid when we think about the way that democratic decision-making works in the United States. While the

Establishment Clause expresses a deep commitment to the individual's right to be free of religious coercion, each citizen is also free to influence leadership and policy based on whatever rationale he or she finds most reliable. In the United States, religion supplies the values that many hold dear, the "strong evaluations . . . discriminations of right and wrong, better or worse, higher and lower, which are not rendered valid by our own desires, inclinations, or choices, but rather stand independent of these and offer standards by which they can be judged."[18] Thus, when it comes to the debate about issues such as abortion, contraception, health care, the death penalty, euthanasia, stem-cell research, same-sex marriage, science education in the public schools, climate change, economic inequality, and so many others, religion's "strong evaluations" come into play. In addition, many Americans apply the same principles when they elect their leaders, and these leaders in turn claim that their own religious orientation influences their decisions and policies. To understand where Americans are coming from and why they make the choices they do—from the average citizen to the occupant of the White House—we need to take account of religion.

Because of America's persistent and continually developing multicultural identity, understanding religion in the United States now overlaps significantly with *global* religious literacy. But there are some unique forms in the United States that should draw our attention. The dual commitment to individual rights and free exercise enshrined in the First Amendment, for example, is reflected in a class of Americans that sociologist Wade Clark Roof called "seekers."[19] Seekers distrust organized religion, and yet they recognize that the meaning provided by traditional ideas and rituals is desirable and necessary; they want to believe and practice, but they don't necessarily want to belong. Hence they often call themselves "spiritual," as in, "I'm spiritual, but not religious," and they construct their own, individually tailored worldviews.

The seeker raises important issues about the adaptability of religious forms, the American commitment to individualism, and the role of syncretism (the combination of beliefs and practices from different traditions) as a factor in religious change. Recently scholars have taken note of another emerging group that is an update on the "seeker" category: "nones." Recent polls show that almost one in five American adults now responds to questions about religious affiliation by saying "none,"[20] prompting one scholar to proclaim that "the rise of the 'nones' surely suggests it is the end of religion as we know it."[21] While this declaration is perhaps a bit dramatic—institutional, organized religion is still alive and well, even in the United States, and (importantly) around the world—the rise of the "nones" is indeed a fascinating trend.

But change is nothing new to American religion, even in its more institutionalized forms. American organizations and congregations have been characterized by both creativity and diversification. Denominations and churches constantly split, combine, and recombine; new sects spring up, sometimes driven by charismatic leaders who reconfigure belief and practice according to their own idiosyncratic inspirations, or in reaction to the perceived threat of liberalizing, secular influences. On the one hand, the proliferation of New Religious Movements (NRMs), which scholars sometimes categorize by "family" (e.g., Latter-Day Saint/Mormon, Communalist, Psychic/New Age, Magical/Pagan, Eastern, and Middle Eastern),[22] is a testament to American tolerance. On the other hand, some of these groups have tended to isolate themselves from mainstream American society, often under the direction of charismatic or even authoritarian leaders who demand strict obedience and absolute devotion. Many would call these groups "cults"—and this is where American tolerance has at times reached its limit.

The "free exercise" principle in the Constitution permits these groups to exist, but when the tension between the insular world of these communities and mainstream society (or government authorities) becomes too great, there is a flashpoint, as was the case in Jonestown, where 900 members of the People's Temple died by suicide and murder in 1978, or in Waco, where over seventy members of the Branch Davidian group were killed in the midst of a government assault in 1993. Why do people join these groups? What power do their leaders have? When do they cross the line and become something civil society cannot tolerate? What do they tell us about the nature of religion? The American experience will continue to include these groups, and so these questions will certainly persist.

"[President Obama's second inaugural address] began with a powerful image: America is on a journey, a perpetual pilgrimage, never arriving at a settled place . . . Journey is not only a biblical image. It is a central theme to many faiths: the Buddhist seeking enlightenment; a Native American on a vision quest; a Muslim embarked on the Hajj;

a Jew hoping for "next year in Jerusalem" at Passover; a Catholic visiting a shrine; a Protestant tracing the footsteps of Martin Luther; a Wiccan making a way to Stonehenge; a humanist celebrating Thomas Jefferson at Monticello. We are a nation of spiritual migrants and immigrants, a restless sort of people, on innumerable sojourns paying homage to our saints and heroes, always searching out new meaning in the universe we inhabit."[23]

Diana Butler Bass

"Mainstream popular imagination has tended to view such [cultic, sectarian, or marginal religious] movements through the lens of exteriority, and the primary models available to the imagination for interpreting, making sense of, and coming to terms with exteriority have been the asylum and the prison. Alternative religious movements, therefore, tend to register within this imagination of otherness as either "crazy," "criminal," or usually both."[24]

David Chidester

When it comes to a nation's relationship with its religious past and present, America is a complex, intriguing case. Like most other countries, the history of the United States is intimately connected with religion (Christianity in particular), but it has become a home to the full range of global traditions, to a wide variety of movements, and to non-traditional perspectives, as well as irreligious ones. Here we have only scratched the surface, but once again, we see the overarching point: to understand America, you have to understand its religion.

"[I]t might well be said that one's education is not complete without a study of comparative religion or the history of religion and its relationship to the advancement of civilization . . . Nothing we have said here indicates that such study of the Bible or of religion, when presented objectively as part of a secular program of education, may not be effected consistent with the First Amendment."[25]

Tom Clark, US Supreme Court Justice
(*Abington v. Schempp*, 1963)

## Turning to You, the Student

So far we have considered the big picture, the national and international scenes. But studying religion is not *just* about why someone out there, off in some other place, does what he or she does. And it is not *just* about providing context for the grand issues that grip our world. It is also necessarily about *us*.

Sometimes the impulse behind studying religion in an academic setting is personal and relatively straightforward. It is not unusual to find Hindus in classes on Hinduism, Jews studying Judaism, Christians enrolled in classes on the New Testament, and so on. Students—and scholars—are often interested because they want to know more about their own tradition, especially in comparison with others. This rationale is most often welcomed in the religious studies classroom, but, of course, you do not need to be religious or come from a religious background to study religion. In fact, *this academic field promotes fundamental understanding of both oneself and others, and thus it is relevant for everyone.* As discussed in preceding pages, we are talking about a public, social phenomenon associated with beliefs and practices that are intertwined with other areas of human concern. To learn about it is to learn about a form of life and social factor that is preeminent for most of our fellow human beings.

But there other issues at stake, and one might say that they are the most important. It's worth asking yourself: *Why, ultimately, does this kind of inquiry matter?* And here's another answer, one that overlaps with goals of a well-rounded education in general: *In studying religion, we inevitably brush up against the big questions that concern all of us.* Who or what am I? What is the most important thing in life? What is the right way to live? What is the right thing to do? What is most true and reliable: The products of our mind? Our feelings? A text? An experience? Are we free to choose our fate, or has it been predetermined? Why is there suffering in the world, and can we do anything about it? What is the meaning of life and death? Is there something beyond this level of reality? Are there higher powers that stand outside our world—or maybe within it—and somehow direct it? And so on. When we read about, observe, and talk with those who live out religious responses to these questions, we also think about our *own* responses to them, and thus we learn something vitally important about ourselves.

So this area of investigation helps us apprehend how others live, contextualize big issues, gain insight on the big questions, and acquire self-knowledge, whether we happen to be religious or not. To get the full benefit of this enterprise, however, we must be focused and methodical — and that is primarily what this book is about. Four interrelated principles provide our starting point. They offer initial guidance in establishing ourselves as observers of the data, smoothing the way for effective analysis of what's "out there." And also, from the outset, they encourage a reflective attitude that provides a window into our own sensibilities. These basic methodological principles are *self-consciousness, comparison, defamiliarization,* and *empathy*.

## Self-Consciousness

It is safe to say that religion means something to everyone, simply because everyone has some experience with it. Some of us come from a religious background; others do not or have moved away from it. But all of us have preconceived notions: these generic terms "religion" and "religious" that we keep throwing around elicit associations and recall past experience. When we try to understand anything, especially something this complex, it is necessary to get clear on where we stand. Every beginning student comes to the subject with "baggage," and we need to come to terms with it.

At this point, pause in your reading. *Where are you starting from?* Do you come from a religious background, or not? What expectations about religion do you have? What do you think about religion in general, or about religious forms that are different from your own? How might your own experience color the way you look at others? These are difficult questions, requiring long and thoughtful answers, but you can perhaps bring them into focus by imagining a conversation with the following "types":

- A skeptical atheist, the son or daughter of two scientists.
- An evangelical Christian who believes that the Bible is the literal word of God.
- Another Christian whose life in the church has led her to join social and political movements opposing racial discrimination and economic injustice.
- A "New Age" child of "hippies" who believes in spirituality but not organized religion.
- A Jewish student who observes on Yom Kippur and Passover, but generally doesn't go to synagogue.

- A black belt in karate who has begun to subscribe to the tenets of Zen Buddhism.
- The child of a mixed marriage between a lapsed Catholic and a self-proclaimed "cultural Jew."
- A student from a generally Christian/Protestant background whose family never really took going to church or religion all that seriously.
- Someone who grew up in a Catholic family, went to Catholic school and, while remaining Catholic, is somewhat ambivalent about the whole experience.
- A nature lover who is unaffiliated with any particular religion, but gets into the outdoors as much as she can because of its intense beauty and calming serenity.
- A Hindu who is used to having an altar devoted to several gods in his family home, but he believes that all religions are essentially teaching the same message.
- A Muslim committed to following the will of Allah: she can't understand Christianity with its Trinity and three gods in one.

Obviously these examples are selective and simplified, but we can use them to imagine just how much a person's background might affect the way he or she views the data. What will the committed monotheist think when encountering people worshiping in a polytheistic tradition—and vice versa? Won't a literalist from one tradition have a hard time comprehending the meaning of another's scriptures? What does a committed atheist bring to the table, and what about someone whose experience with religion has been, at best, mixed? What about those who are only mildly religious, who prefer that it not interfere too much with their lives? Of course, these questions could go on and on, but they point to a fundamental axiom: *Acknowledge your biases and preconceptions at the beginning of any attempt to understand the beliefs and practices of others.*

There are different schools of thought about what to do with background assumptions once we have highlighted them. A *phenomenological* approach urges us to "bracket" assumptions so our object of study can appear as it is, without any filters. Here's an example: If a Protestant Christian wants to study religion, she must set aside her prior judgments and assumptions, and only then can she properly observe other traditions. So if the Protestant student goes looking for a *Bible* in each tradition that she encounters (because the Christian Bible is such a focal point in her own worldview), she will often be frustrated or misled. What is the

"Bible" of Shintoism, or of an Australian aboriginal community? Are there scriptures in Buddhism or Hinduism that are like the Bible in the Christian tradition? Some traditions don't have a single, authoritative anthology; some don't have written scriptures at all. Some have vast open-ended scriptural collections; some revere a single, very concise book or text. In addition, the level of authority accorded to scripture varies from tradition to tradition, as does the nature of commentary that is applied to it. In sum, Christian assumptions about what scripture is (or should be) often do not fit. For the phenomenologist of religion, it is necessary to put aside such assumptions and take things on their own terms. Only then can we be open to observing the data as it really appears, which in turn provides the basis for higher-order categorization and analysis.

Despite its promise to remove our biases, however, the phenomenological approach is not uncontroversial. Is it possible to be *completely* objective, to leave all of our "baggage" behind, even if we try our best to do so? Don't we always have assumptions when we study something? Aren't we always already involved in what we're examining, as soon as we start looking at it? A different approach that assumes we cannot in fact be totally objective is *hermeneutical* in orientation. Understanding begins, according to this method, when we put our prior judgments and assumptions out there and then test them against what we encounter. In this case, instead of *bracketing* our background, we should allow it to *come forth* as the starting point. So the Protestant Christian asks Protestant Christian questions about other traditions and realizes that some of the questions fit and many of them do not; then she adjusts her approach to become more precise. For our hypothetical Protestant student, scripture and thence the Bible may seem to be an obvious place to begin in examining non-Christian religions. But upon discovering that most traditions don't have "Bibles," that scripture takes a wide variety of forms and possesses a wide range of authority, the hermeneutical method insists that this observer must adjust her investigation accordingly— and continually. The model for the hermeneutical method is dialogue, an in-depth back-and-forth between inquirer and subject matter that results in a heightened, but always approximate, level of understanding.

These two approaches are in most ways quite different. The phenomenological method requires that we set aside our background assumptions in order to let the data shine through; it suggests that the best observer is neutral, stable, and somewhat detached. In contrast, the hermeneutical method proposes that understanding only happens when we are willing to put prior judgments into play; the ideal student enters into a conversation with the data and allows her position as observer not only to get involved, but also to change. But there is common ground here. In both cases we are urged to be methodologically self-conscious when studying religion, to clarify our own background and biases, so as to eliminate as many distortions as possible. This fundamental procedure improves our perception of the worldviews of others, and it also inevitably teaches us about ourselves.

"The term *epoche* . . . implies that no judgment is expressed concerning the objective world, which is thus placed "between brackets", as it were. All phenomena, therefore, are considered solely as they are presented to the mind, without any further aspects such as their real existence, or their value, being taken into account; in this way the observer restricts himself to pure description systematically pursued, himself adopting the attitude of complete intellectual suspense, or of abstention from all judgment, regarding these controversial topics."[26]

Gerardus van der Leeuw

"The essence of the question is to open up possibilities and keep them open. If a prejudice [a prior judgment about something we interpret] becomes questionable in view of what another person or text says to us, this does not mean that it is simply set aside and the text or the other person accepted as valid in its place . . . In fact our own prejudice is properly brought into play by being put at risk. Only by being given full play is it able to experience the other's claim to truth and make it possible for him to have full play himself."[27]

Hans-Georg Gadamer

## Comparison

*Comparison* is also a vital tool that contributes to knowledge of both self and others. Max Müller, a prominent nineteenth-century scholar, established one of the most basic principles in the study of religion: "He who knows one, knows none."[28] Understanding moves forward, Müller argued, with discernment of similarities and differences. If we want to appreciate what makes one form of music or art or cuisine what it is, for example, we have to compare it with others. If we wish to analyze a current event, then we compare it with previous episodes in history to see what can be learned. If we want to choose a candidate or policy to support, then we compare with the alternatives. And on it goes: *comparison is an indispensable tool for identifying, clarifying, and ultimately understanding any given object of inquiry.*

So in order to gain insight into religious phenomena, Müller argued, we must compare. And taking one step further, our *own* worldview is not truly comprehensible without comparative study. Many scholars—especially but not exclusively phenomenologists—have pursued the comparative study of religion with an eye toward both broad patterns and fruitful contrasts. Is it possible that there are common, archetypal patterns that manifest themselves in many, or all religions? Only by collecting data and making comparisons could we possibly make that case. On the other side of the ledger, what makes a particular religious practice, or an entire tradition, unique? Contrasting it with others leads to answers. Whether we emphasize similarity or difference, comparative analysis is a powerful operation for discerning the significance—perhaps even the very essence—of what we observe.

For Müller, however, comparison was also a necessary component of self-understanding, and thus he also presaged the hermeneutical approach. He went so far as to say that the adherent of any given tradition just doesn't understand it if he or she fails to study others. In order to grasp this part of the comparative principle, recall that old maxim, "Ignorance is bliss." It is tempting to enclose oneself within a worldview, refusing exposure to any others, so as to avoid challenges—and that goes for religious and nonreligious people alike. Absent comparison, contrast, and broader perspective, our understanding of and commitment to our own worldview is incomplete. It's like tasting one flavor of ice cream (or perhaps tasting it over and over again and knowing it very well and also being completely in love with it) and then proclaiming that one knows what flavored ice cream in general is all about. Pushing Müller's idea even further, adherence to one way of life, without comparison, is an empty gesture. How can we know that our way is the best, without vigorous comparison with other possibilities? And without that comparative analysis, how can we consider our commitments genuine and authentic?

At the very least, comparison accompanies self-consciousness as a basic method in the study of religion. Recognizing that one thing is similar to or the same as something else, or discerning that things are different from each other—these are basic intellectual operations that lead into more sophisticated forms of analysis and, at times, unexpected flashes of insight.

> "The process of comparison is a fundamental characteristic of human intelligence . . . comparison, the bringing together of two or more objects for the purpose of noting either similarity or dissimilarity, is the omnipresent substructure of human thought. Without it, we could not speak, perceive, learn, or reason . . . That comparison has, at times, led us astray there can be no doubt; that comparison remains the method of scholarship is likewise beyond question."[29]
>
> Jonathan Z. Smith

## Defamiliarization

A principle that extends on comparison in religious studies is called *defamiliarization*: "making the familiar seem strange in order to enhance our perception of the familiar."[30] Defamiliarization also has an inverse—making the strange seem familiar—which we will discuss below. So how does this two-sided operation work?

To get a handle on this idea, think about movies that make the familiar strange by challenging our usual perception of things. In *The Matrix* (1999), for example, the world that we think we know actually turns out to be a computer-generated illusion; the reality is that we are all encased in cocoons, and machines are using our inert bodies to produce energy. In this case, the film compels us to see our usual experience and beliefs in a very different light—it is virtual, only as real as a video game. After seeing a film like this for the first time, we wonder—if only for a few minutes—about whether the world of our senses is "really there." That's defamiliarization: its effect is to question the reliability of our most basic beliefs. Other recent films that use this method to great effect include *Memento* (2000), *Minority Report* (2002), *Eternal Sunshine of the Spotless Mind* (2004), and *Inception* (2010).

In applying this principle to the study of religion, it should be noted from the outset that defamiliarization does not entail tearing down religious worldviews by making them seem "weird" just for the sake of it. Instead, the objective is "to enhance our perception of the familiar" by shaking things up a bit and seeing what happens. Recalling our example from the earlier section on self-consciousness, many see the Christian Bible as a "book," a unified product of divine revelation. Fair enough, but defamiliarization would begin with an acknowledgment of the huge range of materials in this anthology, and recognition that there are different voices, anomalies, and even seeming contradictions that appear in its pages. So here's a defamiliarizing hypothesis: if we look at the Bible in a certain way, it appears as if an editor (or group of editors) collected a bunch of disparate sources, stitched them together, and then presented the end-product as a unified whole. So it's not really a "book"; it's more like a magazine, or a mash-up. And this way of looking at it leads to the broader point: recognizing the diversity of perspectives contained in the Bible forces us to take another look at something that previously seemed stable, and this in turn leads to a more nuanced understanding of the history and development of the communities that revere this text.

Let's move beyond texts and consider another example. Many Christians who come to the academic study of religion for the first time think that they have a pretty good idea of what their tradition is all about. But defamiliarization sets in when they encounter the tremendous variety of forms that Christianity has taken. A devout medieval woman imagines herself as the bride of Christ, sleeping with his corpse in the grave. The Filipino man allows himself to be crucified on Good Friday—with real nails driven into his hands and feet. Appalachian Christians handle poisonous snakes to show their faith, inspired by one verse in the New Testament. Mystics and monks seek out the contemplative life, retire from the world, and take lengthy (or life-long) vows of silence. Citing the model of the early community, Christians have chosen radically communal forms of life; they have also chosen lives of wealth, opulence, and/or radically individual paths of self-fulfillment. The variety goes beyond ancient versus modern, or Protestant versus Catholic versus Orthodox; it is made up of a multitude of divergent beliefs, practices, communities, and personalities.

A final example, now with contemporary American culture in mind. For plenty of Americans, what is normal and familiar is a relatively nonreligious form of life, a largely secular existence. But it is worth highlighting a set of public rituals that many citizens perform, rituals that seem to offer "a genuine apprehension of universal and transcendent religious reality . . . as revealed through the experience of the American people"—singing "God Bless America" at a baseball game, for example, or an athlete praising or thanking God after a major success.[31] Examples such as these defamiliarize the "secular." Perhaps secular life goes under the guise of being irreligious, but it also contains traces of the religious that still in fact serve as its basis. Or, indeed, as some have proposed, religion really *is* on its way out, if for many people it only makes its presence known in these watered-down expressions. Coming to a conclusion on this matter would require a lot of thought and research, but at the most basic level, this example leads us to question something that formerly seemed obvious: the common distinction between religious and nonreligious spheres.

In sum, defamiliarization is a methodological operation that spins off of comparison; it's a matter of taking the things that we think we know and putting them alongside others that seem radically disparate or incongruous. Thereby we get some perspective on the familiar so we can look at it from a very different angle. Then we pay close attention to the results of this operation and attempt to make sense of them within a more sophisticated framework. In essence, defamiliarization serves as a constant reminder that things are rarely as simple as they first seem.

## Empathy

The inverse of defamiliarization would be to make the strange familiar, and this is a first step of yet another basic methodological operation: *empathy*. Empathy first requires study and knowledge of worldview (familiarity with it). But to understand it truly, another step is necessary: we have to "walk a mile in someone else's moccasins," as prominent scholar of religion Ninian Smart was fond of saying. We have to take on the worldview imaginatively and, for a time, try it on for size.

Empathy is of course a feature of everyday life. It emerges in a variety of situations (e.g., comforting a friend in need, trying to understand an alternative viewpoint in a discussion or debate, and so on). And like defamiliarization, it makes regular appearances as a motif in both high art and popular culture. In the 2009 film *Avatar*, for example, a soldier from earth, Jake Sully, has his personality and consciousness transferred into the body of a ten-foot tall blue humanoid creature—a Na'vi—from the planet Pandora. The plan is for him to infiltrate the Na'vi and provide information to the military that will help in conquering them. In his avatar, Jake learns the ways of the Na'vi. Eventually he adopts their worldview and interests fully. At the end of the film, after turning his back on the members of his own species and in fact fighting with the Na'vi against them, Jake permanently transfers himself into the alien body—which now becomes his, along with the culture that he has adopted.

Of course, this is a rather literal (and extreme) example of empathy. Jake has the advantage of *actually* being able to walk—at first temporarily, and then as a permanent condition—in the shoes of the other. And in the end, he decides not to return to his own life and people. So perhaps we should shift the focus to ourselves as viewers of a film like this. Here, the audience obviously does not (and cannot) have Jake's experience, but by means of it, it is possible to identify with the Na'vi. When we begin to understand their perspective and perhaps identify with their values and causes—even though they fight, in some sense, against "us" (human beings)—we engage in an act of the *empathetic imagination*.

The student of religion also engages in this familiar activity, just in a more structured and methodical way. As we find in *Avatar*, it begins with acquainting oneself with the "facts" of another person's tradition (beliefs, sacred stories, key rituals, etc.) and might also build on discovering some similarity and agreement. But the key to empathy is seeing the world as another individual does with neutrality (i.e., lack of judgment) and with all of the difference or "strangeness" of that perspective intact.

Let's work through an example. Imagine an American student in a religious studies class whose goal is to understand the worldview of a monk within the Theravada branch of Buddhism (the form that is prevalent in Sri Lanka and parts of Southeast Asia). This student comes from a Catholic background but generally lives a nonreligious life and is very interested in pursuing a career in business. Where is the starting point? The idea of the monasticism is perhaps familiar (she went to Catholic school and was taught by nuns), as is the emphasis on compassion that both Buddhism and Catholicism share. Some Theravada Buddhists also reinforce a message of self-reliance and common sense, and this might also resonate with our hypothetical student's practical side.

So these moments of recognition provide an opening . . . but the process of cultivating empathy immediately becomes more challenging. To see the world as the Theravadan monk does, for example, this student must undertake a significant shift in perspective. For example, the monk believes in reincarnation, the notion that we are continuously born and re-born, taking on different forms in one lifetime after the next. The monk also denies the existence of a single God who rules over the universe and ultimately provides salvation to his devotees. The monk also has a highly structured, anti-materialistic existence: he begs for his food, sleeps on a hard bed, does not handle money, avoids entertainment and self-adornment of all kinds, and may live a solitary life in forest retreat. While the similarities initially pave the way to empathetic engagement, to take on this alternative perspective is quite challenging. What would it be like to walk this monk's path and see the world with his eyes, for a day, even for an hour?

Empathy is difficult, but it is essential for any committed student of religion. With enough openness and knowledge, it is in fact possible to see the world as another does—if only partially and temporarily. A heightened degree of comprehension and insight is the result. And this is the main purpose behind all of these methodological principles: they put observers of religion in a better position to understand and interpret this complex subject matter. These steps make us better observers, but they also teach us about ourselves, by identifying our "baggage," by requiring useful comparisons, by challenging our assumptions about what we think we know, by calling us forth to see the world as others do. We should not forget that these principles are also about us, we who study religion, and our own self-understanding.

## Dwelling in a World of Meaning

We began this chapter by reflecting on a provocative counterpoint: maybe religion is on the way out, so perhaps it's time to let it go as an object of study and move on. There's much that disputes this contention, however, as religion continues to be a powerful and pervasive reality. This investigation is a study in meaning, as you'll recall from J. Z. Smith's statement, quoted in the Preface: "What we study when we study religion is one mode of constructing worlds of meaning, worlds within which men [and women] find themselves and in which they choose to dwell." That so many of our fellow human beings continue to dwell in these worlds would perhaps surprise figures such as Nietzsche and Freud if they caught a glimpse of our time, and yet they could not deny what they saw.

This chapter has also begun to suggest that this academic field is itself a distinct "world of meaning" for you, the student. That may be most obvious when there is something immediate at stake: that is, you are religious yourself, and you want to gain insight into your own background through in-depth study and comparative analysis. But meaning and significance are present even if this is not the case for you. On a number of different levels, the examination of religion has relevance for all of us. By means of the basic methodological principles we have explored above (self-consciousness, comparison, defamiliarization, and empathy), not only do other forms of life begin to come into focus, but they provide the foundation for the study of religion as a secure academic dwelling place of its own.

# Notes

1. Friedrich Nietzsche, *The Gay Science*, trans. Walter Kaufmann (New York: Vintage Books, 1974), 181.
2. Emile Durkheim, *The Division of Labor in Society*, trans. W. D. Halls (New York: The Free Press, 1984), 120.
3. Sigmund Freud, *The Future of an Illusion*, trans. James Strachey (New York and London: W. W. Norton, 1961), 43.
4. Daniel C. Dennett, *Breaking the Spell: Religion as a Natural Phenomenon* (New York: Viking, 2006), 17.
5. "Remarks at the Launch of the Office of Faith-Based Community Initiatives." http://www.state.gov/secretary/remarks/2013/08/212781. htm.
6. *Global Index of Religion and Atheism: Press Release,* WIN-Gallup International, 2012, 2. http://redcresearch.ie/wp-content/uploads/2012/08/ RED-C-press-release-Religion-and-Atheism-25–7–12.pdf.
7. "The Global Religious Landscape." http://www.pewforum.org/2012/12/18/ global-religious-landscape-exec/.
8. "Religious Hostilities Reach Six-Year High." http://www.pewforum. org/2014/01/14/religious-hostilities-reach-six-year-high/.
9. Bernard Lewis, "The Roots of Muslim Rage," *The Atlantic Monthly* 266 (September 1990): 60.
10. Sam Harris, *The End of Faith: Religion, Terror, and the Future of Reason* (New York and London: W. W. Norton, 2005), 109–10.
11. "Views of Muslim-Americans Hold Steady after London Bombings." http:// www.pewforum.org/2005/07/26/views-of-muslim-americans-hold-steady-after-london-bombings/.
12. "Muslims Widely Seen as Facing Discrimination." http://www.pewforum. org/2009/09/09/muslims-widely-seen-as-facing-discrimination/.
13. *Terror in the Mind of God: The Global Rise of Religious Violence*, 3rd ed. (Berkeley and Los Angeles: University of California Press, 2003).
14. The following scheme is derived from Bruce Lincoln, "Conflict," in *Critical Terms for Religious Studies*, ed. Mark C. Taylor (Chicago and London: University of Chicago Press, 1998), 57–65.
15. "Report 2: Religious Beliefs & Practices/Social & Political Views." *Religious Landscape Survey*. http://religions.pewforum.org/reports#.
16. In a 2013 Harris Interactive poll, belief in God had slipped to 74 percent, and 19 percent of Americans described themselves as "very religious," 40 percent as "somewhat religious." "Americans' Belief in God, Miracles

and Heaven Declines." http:www.harrisinteractive.com/NewsRoom/ HarrisPolls/tabid/447/ctl/ReadCustom%20Default/mid/1508/ ArticleId/1353/Default.aspx.

17. William Scott Green, "The Difference Religion Makes," *Journal of the American Academy of Religion* 62, no. 4 (Winter 1994): 1193.

18. Charles *Taylor, Sources of the Self: The Making of Modern Identity* (Cambridge, MA: Harvard University Press, 1989), 4.

19. See *A Generation of Seekers: The Spiritual Journeys of the Baby Boom Generation* (San Francisco: HarperCollins, 1993).

20. See "Americans and Religion Increasingly Parting Ways, New Survey Shows," UC Berkeley News Center, March 12, 2013. http://newscenter. berkeley.edu/2013/03/12/non-believers/.

21. Gary Laderman, "The Rise of Religious 'Nones' Indicates the End of Religion as We Know It," *Huffington Post*, March 30, 2013. http://www. huffingtonpost.com/gary-laderman/the-rise-of-religious-non_b_2913000. html.

22. This typology is drawn from J. Gordon Melton, "Modern Alternative Religions in the West," in *A Handbook of Living Religions*, ed. John R. Hinnells (London: Penguin Books, 1991), 460–66.

23. "The Obama Doctrine: American Civil Spirituality," *OnFaith*, January 24, 2014. http://www.faithstreet.com/onfaith/2014/01/24/the-obama-doctrine-american-civil-spirituality/30562.

24. David Chidester, *Salvation and Suicide: Jim Jones, the Peoples Temple, and Jonestown*, rev. ed. (Bloomington and Indianapolis: Indiana University Press, 2003), 25.

25. "School District of Abington Township, Pennsylvania v. Schempp" (Cornell University Law School, Legal Information Institute). http://www.law.cornell. edu/supremecourt/text/374/203.

26. Gerardus van der Leeuw, *Religion in Essence and Manifestation*, trans. J. E. Turner (Princeton, NJ: Princeton University Press, 1986), 646.

27. Hans-Georg Gadamer, *Truth and Method*, rev. ed., trans. Joel Weinsheimer and Donald G. Marshall (New York: Continuum, 1994), 299.

28. Max Müller, "The Comparative Study of Religions," excerpt reprinted in *Classical Approaches to the Study of Religion: Aims, Methods, and Theories of Research*, ed. Jacques Waardenburg (New York and Berlin: Walter deGruyter, 1999), 93.

29. Jonathan Z. Smith, "*Adde Parvum Parvo Magnus Acervus Erit*," in *Map Is Not Territory: Studies in the History of Religions* (Chicago and London: The University of Chicago Press, 1993), 240–41.

30. Jonathan Z. Smith, Introduction to *Imagining Religion: From Babylon to Jonestown* (Chicago and London: University of Chicago Press, 1982), xiii.

31. Robert Bellah, "Civil Religion in America," in *Beyond Belief: Essays on Religion in a Post-Traditional World* (Berkeley: University of California Press, 1970), 179.

# 2 Theory in the Field: An Introduction

---

**CHAPTER CONTENTS**

---

In the first chapter of this book we gave some thought to the significance of a thing called "religion," a phenomenon that is central in many people's lives, guiding their views, actions, and decision-making. It is intertwined with pressing issues on the national and international stage, and it exposes big questions that all human beings must face, in one way or another. It therefore captures our attention and calls out for further scrutiny.

The academic study of religion provides a stable position from which to observe, to interpret, and to understand this phenomenon. We have discovered that we are implicated in our examination of this subject matter even before we get started: we're involved in it even *before* we begin, because "religion" already means *something* to us. As a result, it is essential to be methodical and self-aware. Students of religion need to be self-conscious, they must engage in careful comparisons and productive juxtapositions, and they should be ready to imagine their way into the worldview of others, even if that worldview is radically unfamiliar.

But where do we go from here? How can we build on these basic operations to take a *deeper* look, such that the investigation is not just about learning the "facts" about any given tradition or community, but it is also about discerning what this information really *means*? This is where *theory* in the academic study of religion comes in. A theory is a pathway toward examination of that which is not immediately apparent; it is built on evidence, argument, demonstration, and previous track record of usefulness and success. When theories work, as this chapter will show, they contribute to four higher order modes of interpretation and understanding: *definition*, *description*, *explanation*, and *prediction*. These functions are vital in any attempt to take a deeper look at religion, to piece the data together, and to discern its significance.

## Getting into Theory

It should be acknowledged from the outset that the word "theory" might send misleading signals. For some, it is associated with complicated, abstract, perhaps intimidating ideas; it is something that only geniuses can invent or master. On a similar note, the "theoretical" is often considered the opposite of the concrete and the practical, with supposedly little to do with the real world. Some also suggest that "theory" is akin to a hazy, unproven speculation or an opinion, as in the common retort, "Well, that's only a theory."

So what exactly is *theory*? In its origins our word "theory" comes from the ancient Greeks, who associated their word *theoria* with a kind of deep seeing. In other words, a theory is a way of seeing something in order to understand it better, a look beyond surface appearances to see the way something really is. This might sound a little mysterious, but think about how we "theorize" all the time. Often in the midst of everyday discussion and debate, for example, someone will interject, "I have a theory about this." The meaning is clear: the person is saying, "I think I have a better way of understanding what we're talking about. Let me explain." If this "theoretical idea," to use Ivan Strenski's phrase, is well thought out and is based on significant experience and evidence, then it might just offer a more accurate, effective, and insightful way of viewing the issue at hand.

And that, in essence, is what we are after in employing theory in the academic study of religion. As Strenski has written, "Nowhere can the study of religion claim to own anything remotely approaching a Darwinian theory of evolution or a Newtonian theory of the physical universe." And yet our field does share an important assumption with scientific approaches: theories are always subject to testing, both against the data, and by fellow researchers. Because of this kind of evaluation, intuitions can be transformed into "interesting and fruitful theoretical ideas, approaches, 'takes,' or 'angles' with which to approach religion."[1]

To begin to flesh out these points, consider the following example:

About a year ago a young man (let's call him Kurt) started getting into trouble at school. His behavior got worse, leading to angry confrontations with his teachers and the principal. Most recently Kurt expanded his exploits to include vandalizing a police car, and now he's in trouble with the law. Yet he has remained stubborn. When the judge tried to scare him by threatening him with a stay in juvenile detention, Kurt swore at her in open court.

As an old family friend you know something about the back-story. Kurt's father has always been a tough disciplinarian, and you have never seen him show his son any real affection. In response to Kurt's recent behavior he has simply imposed more regulations and punishments. Now the plan is to send the young man away to military school. Meanwhile, Kurt's mother remains on the sidelines (as she has always done), seemingly frightened of the intensity of the struggle between father and son.

What's going on here? What's your hypothesis about this situation? What *theory* best sheds light on it? Obviously you would need a lot more details to feel comfortable making a firm judgment, but just to get things started, what do you think about this hypothesis:

Look, teenage boys always rebel for a while. So that's what Kurt is doing. Don't worry. He'll get over it.

Maybe this is a reasonable suggestion. Often the data supports this hypothesis. But is it adequate for this case? Is the theory behind this statement correct? For one thing, it seems too general, because it does not go very far in describing the exact nature of Kurt's situation. Also, there are many teenage boys who do not rebel, and even if many or most do, they generally don't go as far as Kurt. This analysis also lacks precision in predicting the way things will go in the future, let alone in determining what could be done about the problem. A more precise diagnosis is necessary, based on a more developed theory.

A better explanation might look something like this:

This is a classic psychological struggle. It's his parents. His father was never emotionally supportive; he disciplined his son severely and never showed he loved him. And his mom, she just sits the whole thing out, and all along he wanted her just once to intervene and stand up for him. Now the kid is lashing out at authority figures who stand in for his parents. That's who he's really angry at: his parents. If his dad would just connect with him instead of imposing harsher discipline, and if his mom would just get involved more, he would stop this destructive behavior.

Maybe this observer is just playing reality-TV psychiatrist, but even so, it seems that we are making progress. Why? What makes one hypothesis better than another?

Let's break this second analysis of Kurt's situation down:

1. The second proposal defines the problem first and foremost as psychological. An important aspect of any theory is its ability to define its object and area of inquiry. In Kurt's case, our observer has said, "When certain kinds of data are observed we are dealing with a psychological issue." If upon further examination it was found that the young man had some kind of brain injury, and that it was directly causing his outbursts, the problem would shift immediately from psychological to neurological. That would require different forms of examination and expertise. But if the psychological definition is correct, then a whole range of appropriate theories and associated remedies become available—and prospects are improved for understanding what Kurt is going through.

2. Definition, explanation, and description weave together. In this example, psychological explanation is based on a targeted hypothesis, guided by a certain theory of human development: when parents consistently frustrate the wishes and desires of children during their upbringing, they will displace their anger onto others. Armed with this theoretical idea, a more insightful description of the situation emerges. Is there merit to the explanatory theory and the description that follows in this case? We would have to investigate further (by talking to the young man about his history and his feelings, for example) to find out. At the very least, we have a plausible

and specific hypothesis to work with, which leads to better questions than we would have posed without it.

3. A theory's ability to predict will sometimes be its best testing ground. The theory that suggests that Kurt is displacing his anger leads to the following prediction: if he becomes fully aware of the true source of his frustration and if he manages somehow to come to peace with it, his (self-)destructive behavior will stop. It would naturally be of great interest to the psychological theorist to see if this prediction panned out.

Now how does this brief example relate to theories of religion?

For one thing, while we should not begin by assuming that religion is some kind of maladjustment in need of treatment, it is a *problem* to the extent that it is not always easy to understand. Kurt's situation would be messy, confusing, and complex in real life—and so (often) is religion, at least from the outsider's perspective. Note how the second theory above sheds light on something that is initially perplexing. Good theoretical ideas in the study of religion should do the same thing: a worthy conceptual framework does not oversimplify, but it should clarify and present an eloquent response to complexity and factors that are less than obvious.

Even more importantly, the theory presented above offers a way forward. It clears the way for further questions, hypotheses, testing, feedback, and observation, but in a targeted, attentive manner. Now we can ask Kurt a useful set of questions, for example. And based on his responses, perhaps the second theoretical idea discussed above will be confirmed—it is all about his displaced anger toward his parents. But perhaps it will not, and this a key element in the application of theory in religious studies as well: we must be ready to adjust any given theoretical approach, make use of some parts of it and not others, or even reject it . . . and reach for something new.

So theory begins as an attempt to look at religion differently, to see it more clearly, to get at what's *really* going on. We apply and evaluate any given theoretical idea in an attempt to define, describe, explain, and make predictions about our subject matter. And, if necessary, we adjust or find another strategy. This process is all about improving our understanding and discerning the meaning and significance behind the "facts."

Going back to those concerns that many have about "theory" described above, you will see that theoretical approaches in the study of religion can be complex, but they are hardly either out of your reach, or out of touch with reality. One scholar addresses the issue this way: "Theory . . . is just a bookish synonym for smart."[2] To this extent, theories are the opposite of random guesses and speculations: they are grounded in a community of inquiry, and thus they have a proven ability to ground conversation and promote further, even more complex questioning.

We turn now to a more detailed consideration of the operations that theories are designed to perform: *definition*, *description*, *explanation*, and *prediction*.

## A WORD ABOUT THE WORD "RELIGION"

The English term "religion" has its origins in the Latin word *religio*. The term appears often both in classical literature and in the early Christian writings (many of which were written in Latin). But scholars are somewhat conflicted about the original etymology of the term.

Most tell us that the term comes from a Latin verb *religare*, which means, "to re-tie" or "bind again." In this sense, the term originally refers to the power of a religious tradition to make connections between people, the ability of religion to bind a community together with common creeds and practices.

Others suggest that the term originally comes from the verb *relegere*, "to re-read," "go through again," or "re-collect" in speech or reflection. This etymology would suggest that the term denotes a continual reinterpretation of some foundational source, such as scripture. But it also suggests repetition in actions, perhaps rituals, and constant deliberation.

Finally, a minority view argues that the term was originally allied, via Latin, with an older Greek word, *alegein*, "to heed," "have a care for," or "be careful about." (The negative of this term would be "to neglect.") So religion is about something powerful that demands close attention and constant care.

The correct etymological answer has no authority in dictating the proper use of the term now, but each of these proposals raises interesting questions about what exactly it refers to—each suggests a different definition, and by extension, each implies a different theory.

## Definition

First and foremost, an adequate theory delimits the phenomenon we propose to investigate. In that sense, definition, or the act of drawing boundaries around the subject matter, provides a crucial starting point.

And yet, when it comes to "religion," this is one of the biggest challenges. While the meaning of the term may at first seem to be transparent, especially in everyday usage, further scrutiny reveals just how difficult defining it can be. What is it, after all, that we are talking about? Any answer, as we will see, is fraught with difficulties, but don't give up hope: some definitions are better than others.

With a little bit of reflection, the definitions of religion that seem most obvious quickly fall apart. Consider one of the most common: religion is belief in God or gods that are to be obeyed and worshiped. At first glance, this proposal, which is found in many dictionaries, seems serviceable. Yet if we push a bit, it starts to crumble. The best initial test for any definition is to look for obvious exceptions: if our intuition or common sense tells us that a tradition or a practice is an example of "religion," and yet it does not fit within our definition, then perhaps something is wrong. For example, the seemingly obvious definition above ("religion is belief in God or gods that are to be obeyed and worshiped") runs into a big obstacle: certain branches of Buddhism. Our instincts tell us that Buddhism is in fact a religion, and yet many Buddhists, while acknowledging the existence of gods, find that they distract from the true goal of their tradition. These Buddhists consider the worship of gods tangential, which seems to run afoul of the definition. So does Buddhism not count? Should we ignore big parts of the Buddhist world because they don't fit with the definition? Or is it the definition itself that needs to be adjusted, or maybe even abandoned?

While we are not always aware of it, definitions carry with them a whole series of choices about what is significant, what is worth studying, and what is not. In other words, they include value judgments. If some strands of the Buddhist tradition do not fit our definition, for example, what should we do with them? When something gets cut out of a category, the message is often that it is devalued—in this case, some strands of Buddhism, because belief in God/gods is not central in them. Flawed definitions forcefully exclude or marginalize relevant content, and thus they mislead us about the object of our study—often before we have even gotten started.

It is important to note that even if the content of a tradition falls within a given definition, value judgments are still present. Simplistic definitions have the tendency to identify one aspect of a broader phenomenon as essential, while everything else is peripheral. For example, a prominent scholar of Hinduism (who also happens to come from a Hindu background) has written about being asked to identify the most significant element in her tradition. In one case she said, "Food," because in India, food is a constant element in festivals, rituals, and ceremonies. One of her colleagues responded, "Oh . . . anthropological stuff," and continued by announcing that he was studying "religion" because his area of focus was "the Vedas," the foundational scriptures in the Hindu tradition.[3] As you can see, this response assumes a certain definition, one that makes the distinction between ancient scriptures, which represent "real" Hinduism, and food, which is merely "anthropological stuff."

The difficulties that arise in attempting to define religion might simply speak to a bigger philosophical problem: generalized concepts, no matter how well thought out they are, might never match what they aim to grasp precisely. One great theorist of religion, William James, offered a colorful illustration of this problem: "Probably a crab would be filled with a sense of personal outrage if it could hear us class it without ado or apology as a crustacean, and thus dispose of it. 'I am no such thing,' it would say; 'I am MYSELF, MYSELF alone.'"[4] More recently, Wilfred Cantwell Smith renewed this challenge: "religion," he argued, has become a "thing" in Western intellectual life, "an objective systematic entity"[5] that fails to match up to lived experience and personal faith. Contemporary theorist Jonathan Z. Smith, has his own elegant metaphor for this challenge: "map is not territory." In other words, the diagram that gives us a conceptual or schematic view of the landscape never captures what that territory is really like. It may be that the world simply refuses to bend to our will to categorize and define.

In light of critical arguments like these, some scholars—including W. C. Smith—have recommended that we abandon the term "religion" altogether and thus also the quest for a proper definition of it. But this seems to be a rather extreme response, given the ubiquity of the term and our consistent sense that it does in fact *work* in picking out *something* distinct and meaningful in the realm of human activity and concern. If nothing else, definitions are necessary for further investigation because they locate a starting point and circumscribe the subject matter. If I am very curious about something called "hats," for example, and I want to find out all I can about them, I need a place to begin: "They're the things that human beings put on their heads for comfort, safety, warmth, or adornment." If I do not have some kind of definition to begin with, at least a working one, I might as well give up from the outset—I could end up doing a very long study of shoes, or an intensive examination of sombreros (if my definition was too narrow). I could be missing the forest for one of the trees, or I might be in the wrong wooded area altogether. I need a definitional starting point, even if it gets adjusted and refined based on later findings.

It should also be noted that definitions come in different styles—and perhaps you'll discover that one style suits the subject matter better than another. For example, one type of definition tells us what religion *really* is (in its essence). Scholars have called these definitions *monothetic*: that is, they define religion by a single characteristic (or a very small group of characteristics) that *must* be present for something to be called religion. Monothetic definitions often come in one of two subtypes: definitions that are *substantive* (i.e., they identify the core of religion with a focus on some specific *object*, such as God, gods, powerful beings, power in general, etc.) or *functional* (i.e., they describe religion in terms of what it *does* for human beings—it assuages their fear of death, brings them together socially, reinforces control of one group over another, etc.). Another broad type of definition is *polythetic*: it constructs a list of characteristics that, taken together, describe what religion is generally about. Not all individual instances have all the characteristics, nor is there any one single characteristic that they all must have to be considered "religions." But there is overlap and resemblance among these characteristics—enough to suggest that there is a consistent, continuous reality behind the term, even it cannot be pinned down to one absolute, essential quality.

As you read this book, you will have the opportunity evaluate definitions that come in all of these shapes. Perhaps one of these theoretical ideas will capture your imagination and convince you of its superiority. Perhaps no one definition will persuade you; parts of these ideas will make sense, others won't. And some definitions will strike you as utterly wrong. The key is: this kind of deliberation is central within the academic study of religion, and it reveals the most valuable outgrowth of attempting to *define* something so complex—it's in the deliberation itself, which ultimately leads to more nuanced, insightful analysis.

## Description

We might say that whereas definition emphasizes the general (i.e., religion in general is *this*, or it has this set of characteristics), description focuses on the uniqueness of particulars. As Walter Capps wrote, description marks "the shift from singles to plurals,"[6] or from "religion is x" to examination of its multiple forms. But the two functions are intimately related. Craig

Martin reminds us that "the definition sets out or delimits in advance what the thing is. Only once a thing is delimited can that thing be adequately or inadequately described."[7] So we define in general, delimit our subject and its possible cases, and then dig in and describe.

At first glance, description doesn't seem too complicated. To describe something, don't we just need to observe and record what comes our way? A pencil and notebook (or laptop or tablet) will do, no fancy theories necessary. But maintaining the focus needed to perceive all of the details of any given particular (a ritual, for example) is challenging in itself. And then it should be noted that description intersects with theory as we inevitably interpret what we observe. Real description, even of a single gesture, object, or person, becomes a complex act. Here we will investigate two frameworks for describing religion: phenomenology and "thick description."

In the previous chapter, you were introduced to the phenomenological approach. As you will recall, this method recommends "bracketing" our own perspective in order to let the data appear to us without filters or prior assumptions. Imagine an example of how this process might work. Think of a reluctant student who receives an assignment that he is not at all thrilled about: he is required to observe and then describe people engaging in religious rituals in three different places of worship. If this student proceeds in an anti-phenomenological manner, he will process these experiences according to preconceived notions: "What does the professor want?" "This ceremony goes against what I believe. I find it offensive." "This whole thing doesn't look right or sound good to me. And it's boring." And so on. The descriptions resulting from these judgments will likely be unimpressive. The student gave himself no chance to do phenomenology.

If preconceptions are bracketed, however, the rituals appear just as they are, as worldly data that rush up to us and require careful attention. But the phenomenological attitude requires even more than bracketing one's value judgments: it also asks the observer to suspend his or her "everyday" way of looking at the world. Now think about this: maybe our student goes to the same coffee shop every day, but has he ever stopped to observe the place with great care (the other customers, the sounds, the movements, the patterns, the taste of the coffee, etc.)? Probably not, because the coffee shop is hemmed in by a fixed attitude in his mind: "This is the place where I get coffee (and sometimes get anxious because I'm late for class)." Because the student is in the grip of this habitual thinking, he or she has never done a proper phenomenology of the coffee shop.

The purpose of this kind of bracketing and attention is description of the particulars. So now, after bracketing value judgments and practicing his phenomenological attitude on cafes, our hypothetical student is ready. One afternoon, he visits a Greek Orthodox church, for example, and absorbs everything, through all of the senses, without judgment, without even thinking too much about what he perceives. People come in and make a contribution, light a candle, kiss the icons at the front of the church, and then go on their way. The student describes them: how they look, how they are dressed, how they move, what they seem to express. In the meantime, the student also records the details of the church itself, its colors, scents, sounds, and ambience. In the end our observer has a richly detailed description of this site and what goes on there. His description, theoretically guided by the tenets of phenomenology, will provide the basis for effective analysis and deeper reflection.

Another influential point of reference for description is Clifford Geertz, a prominent American anthropologist who championed an approach called "thick description." In a famous essay on this topic, Geertz begins by telling a story: two boys simultaneously wink at each other, but one is experiencing a nervous twitch, and the other is responding to what he thinks was a secret signal, an actual intentional wink. Now a third boy at the table winks, but he is trying to make fun of the first boy's wink, which was (truth be told) a little awkward. How would we begin to describe and make sense of what has just happened? At the level of "thin description," all three boys have done the same thing by "rapidly contracting . . . right eyelids." But at the level of "thick description," we would have to give an adequate account of what all these gestures really mean—and that would take some doing.[8]

Now think about what it would take to present a "thick description" of a religious event, which in all likelihood would be much more complex than the winking scenario. We would have to maintain attention to detail, and extensive experience with the tradition (and with similar rituals) would enhance the description dramatically. At the same time, a theoretical vocabulary would add texture and depth. As Geertz has suggested, "any effort at thick description" starts "from a general bewilderment as to what the devil is going on," but "one does not start (or ought not to) intellectually empty-handed."[9] He later continues:

A repertoire of very general, made-in-the-academy concepts and systems of concepts—"integration," "rationalization," "symbol," "ideology," "ethos," "revolution," "identity," "metaphor," "structure," "ritual," "world view," "actor," "function," "sacred," and, of course, "culture" itself—is woven into the body of thick-description ethnography in the hope of rendering mere occurrences scientifically eloquent.[10]

The "made-in-the-academy concepts" that Geertz refers to here are similar to (and often the same as) the "theoretical ideas" that scholars put to use in attempting to interpret their subject matter. In this passage, Geertz outlines the way in which description relates to those ideas: preparing for description requires gaining theoretical literacy, and then processing the data is intertwined with a vocabulary that renders our account of it more "scientifically eloquent."

In both cases (phenomenology and "thick description"), theory is interwoven into our ability to absorb and report on specific cases—actions, performances, practices, and representations. To this extent, there is nothing simple about it. And yet description begins with some basics that all of us can cultivate, including openness, attention, and focus. It's rare that we give ourselves the chance to stop and *truly* describe the particulars in life; the academic study of religion, guided by foundational theories and methods, devotes itself to this unique and valuable art.

## Explanation

One of the greatest television series of all time was *The X-Files*. As its episodes unfolded over nine years (1993–2002), a grand mystery was laid out: first, whether extraterrestrials were real and had in fact visited our planet; then, once that first mystery had been settled (they *were* real and lurked everywhere), the main characters (and the audience) needed to figure out what the aliens were up to. Everything on the show called out for explanation: it was all about the intensely human desire to know why things are the way they are.

Religion is *something* like the UFO phenomenon: it presents the mind with a challenge, and many theories have tried to explain it. When it comes to encounters with mysterious lights in the sky, some propose that they are in fact spaceships piloted by extraterrestrials. Others account for them in more down-to-earth ways, suggesting that they are optical illusions, natural phenomena, such as ball lightning, or the product of overactive imaginations. On the one side, the true believers explain UFOs by asserting that there really is something out there (like Fox Mulder from *The X-Files*, who had a poster in his office that proclaimed "I WANT TO BELIEVE"). On the other hand, more cautious or skeptical observers suggest that natural or psychological explanations are simpler and more rational (Mulder's partner, Dana Scully, who was a medical doctor and scientist, constantly brought this perspective to bear).

On *The X-Files*, it was eventually revealed that the true believer was right: UFOs really were alien spaceships. Such a concrete resolution is not to be expected in the academic study of religion. While belief in something that is "really out there" may provide adequate explanation for some, simply "*wanting* to believe" is not nearly enough within the testing ground of academia. So over the past two centuries, the developing social sciences (psychology, sociology, and anthropology in particular) have attempted to fill in the gap by *explaining* religion. From the social scientific perspective, explanatory theories "purport not merely to describe all religions but also to account for them" by identifying "the origin and the function of all religions."[11] In order "to account for" religion, theorists have often been drawn to *genetic* explanations that point to where it first came from historically, or where it comes from whenever it appears. If we can determine why it arose, then we will be able to understand what it is, in its innermost essence, and thus why it persists. The social sciences have also offered an array of *functionalist* theories, framing religion in terms of its purpose for human beings. Of course, genetic and functionalist explanations often go together: if we discover *why* religion first arose, and in response to what basic need, then we will understand its purpose and function.

Critics suggest that this form of explanation often runs into a major problem: *reductionism*. While all theories attempt to explain one thing in terms of another, a reductive theory oversimplifies; it "explains away" a complex reality too quickly. Gavin Flood has identified two main strands of reductionism: (1) within "cultural reductionism," religion is thought to be a delusion "that has served the interests of the rich and the powerful" and (2) within "naturalist or eliminative reductionism," investigating the brain tells us how "cognition and language" work, and "once we know how cognition and language work generally, we can know how religious cognition and language work in particular."[12] As Flood's characterizations suggest, explanatory theories about religion have often been allied with skepticism about it, and a desire to see its illusions dispelled.

And yet explanation does not have to be equated with reductive "explaining away" or subordinated to a preconceived agenda. Can one explanation identify the universal origin and nature of religion? Scholars have dreamed about this possibility and some continue to search—and perhaps you will be inclined to join their quest. Another way of thinking about explanatory theories, however, is more *pluralistic*: no one single explanation will be adequate, so we must instead be ready to see these theories as tools, many of which are helpful indeed in interpreting particular examples.

But no one tool will do for every job. Within a pluralistic approach, the trick is: we must learn to know which tool is appropriate when. Often religious practice is deeply connected with economics, for instance, and needs to be interpreted in those terms. In other instances it is revealed that beliefs are intensely political; they are used to prop up a certain regime or ruling class, for example. In other cases religious fervor resembles what most of us think of as a certain kind of madness: psychological tools must be employed. Devotees retreat from the world and have overwhelming experiences—the experience of the individual needs to be at the center of our analysis. Communal events with a clear social function may also take center stage, so we need to reach for ideas that articulate that function. And, indeed, to understand religion in all of its layers, we need to apprehend it in natural, biological, physiological terms. All of these examples suggest that when it comes to explanatory theories, we must judge on a case-by-case basis, and then reach for the right instrument, recognizing that as useful as it might be, no tool can fix everything at once.

## Prediction

The final function that theory serves is prediction. Being able to predict the future may sound mysterious and prophetic, the province of psychics and media pundits, but it is yet another way that theory is part of your everyday experience. Think about how much of your life depends on both tacit and consciously formed predictions. Based on our knowledge of the natural world, we assume that the sun will come up tomorrow, gauge whether it is safe to cross a street, and have some idea about how the weather will behave. Natural scientists have refined these everyday predictions, based on tried and true theory and method, and they can be quite precise in their prognostications about how the material world will behave.

Of course, *human* behavior on both grand and local scales is more difficult to predict. For this reason, perhaps, prediction is often deemphasized in favor of description, explanation, and, more generally, interpretation in the study of religion. In comparing the interpreter of culture to a doctor, for example, Clifford Geertz suggested that both focus on "the unapparent import of things" in order to make a diagnosis, not a prediction.[13] But at the same time, for a doctor, delivering a *prognosis* is equally important. On a fundamental level, the study of religion attunes us to stable structures in religious traditions, such that we become aware of what will likely happen in any given context, and we know (with a reasonable degree of certainty) what things will mean to practitioners, even in circumstances that seem chaotic and spontaneous to the untrained eye.

Consider the following example. Imagine a "cult" group with about 200 members, including about fifty children, has holed itself up in a compound somewhere in the Western United States. Their leader is a charismatic young man who preaches the Bible for hours on end while his flock sits in rapt attention. Say that the local municipality wants to send in a health inspector, to make sure that the kitchen and sanitary facilities at the ranch are in order. Because of his mistrust of outsiders, the leader refuses to let the inspector in. The police arrive, and a stand-off ensues, especially once the authorities realize that the group is heavily armed. After a few tense days, agents of the federal government appear, and they cut off the electricity and water supply, hoping to force the group out. Then they start bombarding the complex with light and noise during the night-time hours in an attempt to deprive the group members of sleep. Finally, after eighteen days, out of concern for the welfare of the children, the federal agents storm the building. When they make their way to the central common room of the complex, they find all 200 members of the group dead or dying from poison, which they took—or were forced to take—as soon as the attack began.

Obviously the federal agents failed to predict this outcome. They did not want everyone to die (especially the innocent children), but they proceeded on the hypothesis that the leader was a madman who had in effect taken "hostages." Because they were simply "brainwashed" by an unstable personality, law enforcement predicted that if the group was put under some stress, members would begin to defect in large numbers, leaving only the leader and his most loyal henchmen isolated and vulnerable. But this prediction and the theory behind it were tragically wrong. Later it comes out that a religion scholar from the local university had been observing the standoff for its whole duration, and in its early stages he started to do research on the theology of this community and its leader. One day he decided to visit the site himself, and as soon as he saw that the compound was in fact under siege, he had to speak out to the agents leading the investigation. After days of phone calls, he finally was able to meet with the agent in charge.

First he reminded the agent that distinctive patterns were at work in this situation: it was not simply a hostage situation. He argued that the orientation of the people inside meant that they were absolutely fixated on the sacred, something not of this world, something radically distinct from the profane, the secular, the everyday. The members' adherence to this principle, he proposed, came from a deep need for connection and belonging in a world from which they, as individuals, had become alienated. They had sated this hunger by belonging to the sect, but it simultaneously intensified their distance from the outside world. In fact, they had learned to become afraid of its corruption and impurity. Because it had been purified by the group's leader, who was considered to be a man of God, the inside of the compound was "clean," while the outside world was sinful and dirty.

Then the professor described the theology and practices of the group in detail for the agent. To put it briefly, he brought to bear all his experience and theoretical ideas pertaining to apocalyptic groups, or those who tend to see the end of the world—or their departure from it—as imminent. The leader's long speeches pointed to the book of Revelation and linked his own plight and the trials of his group to the end-time described there. He began to interpret the siege by the federal government in these terms, and each new form of pressure was retrofitted to his biblical interpretation. Apocalyptic groups, the scholar suggested, often have an intense distrust of the outside world, and especially secular authorities. They also tend to maintain a dualistic philosophy, where the body and the soul are radically distinct. They propose that when the end comes, or when their end comes, they will be rescued and brought to a better place, and their death would be a message from God to the world and a tribute to his glory. In other words, groups like this readily become martyrs. The scholar concluded (based on definition, explanation, and description) that if the agents continued to apply pressure, many of its members would commit suicide to achieve their goal—and they would force the children to do the same. As the scholar revealed later, the agent remained locked into his own hypothesis about the group's members being standard, run-of-the-mill hostages, and days later the standoff ended in disaster.

This "hypothetical" scenario is of course a composite of the Jonestown episode in 1978, during which over 900 members of the People's Temple committed mass suicide or were murdered, and the occurrences at Waco in 1993, where 74 members of the Branch Davidians died in a fire after the ATF and FBI raided their compound. In the case of Waco, religion scholars actually did attempt to make their predictions known, but to no avail.[14] The example suggests that accumulated experience, good data, and theoretical insight combine to make reasonable predictions possible, even if the powers that be are not willing to listen.

As a beginning student, you probably will not be advising the federal government during tense confrontations. Also, religion has plenty of surprises, making predictions about it quite difficult, as experts will readily admit. And yet you should still think about your knowledge as serving the future: as a family member, friend, neighbor, student, or co-worker, there's no telling when your knowledge may come in handy, not only as a matter of literacy, but also as it relates to making predictions about the way things will go. Additionally, as a citizen, you have a voice about the future as it unfolds: informed judgments can be powerful in our contemporary historical moment, a moment in which religion plays such a significant role.

## Insider/Outsider: Orders of Meaning in the Study of Religion

Everyone knows what it's like to be on the outside. Think about showing up at a party where you don't really know anyone—but everyone there seems to know *each other*. Or maybe you start a new job, or enroll in a new school. Even if you are welcomed in, everyone has his or her fixed patterns and relationships; they have their own way of talking and acting; they know things you don't. Sometimes it takes quite a while to understand what's going on, and then it takes even longer to become an insider.

The academic observer of human culture initially faces a similar problem. Studying a foreign culture in school, for example, is one thing, but encountering it in reality is quite another. Even if we know the language, another land does not give up its secrets easily, and most of us have to work patiently to see it from the inside. Some people take this effort to its extreme: they join the foreign culture; they integrate, assimilate, and "go native," as we saw in the *Avatar* example in the previous chapter.

The academic observer, in contrast, generally wants "in" for the purpose of understanding but also hopes to remain distant enough to be even-handed. This paradox, in which the scholar has a drive to capture the interior of other worldviews but must also remain in some sense aloof, is called the insider/outsider problem.

As you can imagine, religion intensifies this problem, because belonging, being an insider, is often such an emphasis. As we have been describing it, the methodical study of religion involves stepping back; offering defini-tion, descriptions, explanations, and/or predictions; and presenting an analysis or interpretation. Obviously there is a difference between doing these things and living a religion. So if the representations in the field are always going to be *etic* (outsider), how can we be sure that our under-standing is accurate and true to the *emic* (insider)?[15] Would someone have to experience being part of a religious tradition to understand it? Or is distance especially important in studying something like religion, where experiencing its interior would mean . . . becoming religious?

Responding to this dilemma can flow in one of two directions. First: maybe our only way of understanding the insider is to become one, or at least know what it is like to be one; thus having some kind of religious identity or experience oneself is necessary. Short of that, perhaps the researcher's job is to let the insiders do the interpreting (because they are the only ones who really know what they are talking about) and to report on it faithfully. If the student does generate an "outside" interpretation, drawing upon theories and methods from the world of academic inquiry, then the insiders have the final veto power: if those under study cannot assent to it, then the outsider's interpreta-tion must be discounted.

Another, very different response to this matter would suggest that giving the insiders this kind of power defers to them way too much. After all, scholars often know more about the history and variety of traditions they study than people who actually belong to them. Scholars also have distance and perspective; they can compare and analyze using sophisticated intellectual tools. In fact, getting too close to the insiders would be disastrous for the serious researcher: she would lose any kind of scholarly objectivity. And the insiders themselves are not great authorities; they only have their insular perspective. Remember: "he who knows one knows none." If that principle is true, then insiders are actually not in a very good position to talk about their own tradition, let alone religion in general.

Some observers have gone even further in emphasizing the scholar's control. As you will recall from the discussion of definition earlier in this chapter, it may be that the concept "religion" fails to map precisely onto anything "out there." Jonathan Z. Smith has come up with a slogan for this difficulty: "there is no data for religion." Smith writes, "Religion is solely the creation of the scholar's study. It is created for the scholar's analytic purposes by his imaginative acts of comparison and generalization. Religion has no independent existence apart from the academy."[18] While this statement might seem a bit shocking, we recognize that it is really just a splashy way of restating the insider/outsider problem: investigating something called "religion" is always at a distance from its subject matter, because what's "out there" never exactly matches the outsider's conception of it.

"[N]o statement about a religion is valid unless it can be acknowledged by that religion's believers. I know that this is revolutionary, and I know that it will not be readily conceded; but I believe it to be profoundly true and important . . . On the external data about religion, of course, an outsider can by diligent scholarship discover things that an insider does not know and may not be willing to accept. But about the meaning that the system has for those of faith, an outsider cannot in the nature of the case go beyond the believer . . . I would hold emphatically that fruitful study must recognize this principle."[16]

Wilfred Cantwell Smith

"When one permits those whom one studies to define the terms in which they will be understood, suspends one's interest in the temporal and contingent, or fails to distinguish between 'truths', 'truth-claims', and 'regimes of truth', one has ceased to function as a historian or scholar. In that moment, a variety of roles are available: some perfectly respectable (amanuensis, collector, friend and advocate), and some less appealing (cheerleader, voyeur, retailer of import goods). None, however, should be confused with scholarship."[17]

Bruce Lincoln

# Four Orders of Meaning in the Study of Religion

The problem described here is profound, and whether you like it or not, as a student of religion, you are now in the middle of it. But where exactly?

Differentiating "insiders" and "outsiders" further should give you a better idea. There are, in fact, not just "insiders" and "outsiders" in the study of religion: several Orders of Meaning are at work.[19]

1. The First Order, the *immediate*, is constituted by what "insiders" do, say, and feel, while they're in the thick of things religiously. The First Order is made up of "[religious] expression which has often been deemed spontaneous, emotive, and uncritical . . . [It] belongs to the realms of performance and ritual, and to the myth and symbol presumed operative within them."[20] It is also the layer of the text as it is read, recited, or expressed in rituals, ascetic practices, or contemplation.[21] Example: When someone says a prayer, like the Lord's Prayer in the Christian tradition, he or she is present in the moment and in the performance of the ritual; he or she is not busy with intellectual deliberations on the meaning of the prayer. In other words, the practitioner is in the First Order of Meaning, the immediate.

2. The Second Order of Meaning, the *reflective*. Within religious traditions themselves, space is open for reflection on the significance of the immediate order that places it "within the broader scheme of what is deemed to be true."[22] By means of theological, philosophical, commentarial, and legal modes of reflection, a tradition takes a step back from itself and attempts to organize its particular view of the world. Example: In the Christian tradition, theologians, clergy, and educators offer extensive examination of the Lord's Prayer and its meaning for the community: they participate in the Second Order of Meaning, the reflective.

3. The Third Order of Meaning is that of the *academic*: it is the theoretical order that the outside observer occupies as he or she attempts to interpret and understand the other two layers. Example: The function of the Lord's Prayer is to reinforce the social bonds between members of an immediate community (the local church) and the broader community of Christian worshipers (the Christian Church, with capital letters); thus the prayer primarily reinforces a sense of belonging for those who pronounce it. Such interpretations come from an outside, academic perspective, the Third Order of Meaning.

(We should note at this point that the academic, theoretical order of meaning has something in common with the reflective, insider level: both have a tendency to posit a something that stands behind even the First Order, because they claim to have discovered what's really going on. Thus both participants and observers tend to create what we might call a *"Zero Order."* Examples: The Second Order Christian commentator may argue that the Zero Order for the Lord's Prayer is divinely inspired revelation and ultimately God himself. Meanwhile, the Third Order observer claims that what's really going on in the performance of the prayer is a desire for social bonding. All human beings have this need, the hypothetical observer proposes, so the Zero Order is the human brain, which contains a feature, a product of evolution, that reinforces social behaviors.)

4. The Fourth Order of meaning is your particular province: it the *synthetic* order of the student. It "cuts across all the other modes in reflecting the travails of one who must integrate them all in ways that are personally meaningful and communally relevant."[23] As beginning students of religion, you may find yourself, or parts of yourself, on different rungs of this ladder of meaning. How we synthesize these different layers as individuals and understand them when taken together constitutes, for each of us, a Fourth Order of meaning, the synthetic.

This framework gives rise to many challenging questions, but it also clarifies what people do when they discuss and wrestle with religion. Here's an example: Let's say that after you finish reading this book you begin to study Hinduism, and you read some of the scriptures from this tradition, including a text called the *Bhagavad Gita*, which tells the story of a warrior who refuses to fight in a battle against other family members. A god in disguise (Krishna) urges him to fight and eventually appears in his full, divine glory. In the end, the warrior is convinced and starts the war.

Many forms of engaging with the words as they appear on the pages will be located within the First Order of Meaning. A pious person may say them silently to himself; perhaps you go to a temple and see a group of people chanting them in unison. The First Order of Meaning—immediate experiences. Now let's say that in class the professor lectures on the text. He explains the history behind it and provides philosophical context. Where are you now? Generally in the Third Order, right? But the professor is probably also reporting on a fair amount of Second Order reflection from inside the tradition to assist you in understanding the text the way Hindus understand it. Now someone in class says, "I am a Hindu, and in my tradition these words are the authentic teaching of God. I will explain to you why they are authoritative." That clearly seems to be in the Second Order of Meaning. But what if someone responds, "Well, that's all well and good, but this book is actually about keeping an oppressive society in place, keeping the poor people down. That's pretty much what religion in general is all about?" This person is clearly speaking within the Third Order, and he or she has definitely posited a Zero Order of Meaning that stands behind the book: it's really about economics and power.

So here's an interesting question: is it possible to be on several different layers of meaning at once, or to switch between them? Is that desirable, or is it better to pick one order and stick with it? Perhaps you, the student, will begin to assemble a Fourth Order of Meaning. Think about the Hindu student trying, at first, to articulate the significance of the scripture on the reflective level. Maybe she now feels the impact of the Zero Order economic reality that her peer highlighted, and she makes a counter-argument in the language of the Third Order of Meaning, in terms that are not familiar to her tradition: "That Marxian functionalist interpretation is just far too reductive." But then, when she goes to visit her extended family in Delhi the next summer, she repeats verses from the *Gita* with her grand-mother and, for that moment at least, becomes a First Order practitioner of Hinduism once again.

So what is the right response to this complex issue? Who has the authority: insiders or outsiders? Is it acceptable to move back and forth within Orders of Meaning (like the student above)? Can the person locked in the First Order study religion at all? That seems impossible, but can immediate experience be integrated into academic investigation after the fact? Can the Second Order commentator study with neutrality and objec-tivity? Does the Second Order of Meaning sometimes overlap with the Third? Can the Third Order scholar or student ever really understand the interior? Maybe not (depending on what we mean by "understand"), but the broader perspective and intellectual tools of the Third Order observer are in fact indispensable if we hope to acquire balanced information and deeper insights.

So we must be sensitive to and aware of all of these layers as we inter-pret the beliefs, attitudes, and practices that are different from our own. Careful reflection on the "insider/outsider problem" leads beyond a simple duality and into a more subtle analysis of a spectrum or gradation between the inside and the outside. Not all insider activity is the same; no one reflective interpreter holds the key. The Third Order takes up an outside perspective to get a good objective view, but not without some borrowing from other Orders, and not—in many cases—without some active shifting between them in lived experience. In sum, we are drawn back to that crucial methodological point discussed in the previous chapter: bridging some precarious, but not impossible gaps between individuals, cultures, and traditions requires constant vigilance and self-consciousness about where we stand.

## Theology versus Religious Studies

The study of religion puts some unique twists on the insider/outsider problem, but one version of it has caused considerable controversy: What role should theology play in the academic study of religion? When placed side by side in contemporary theoretical discussions, theology and religious studies have taken on distinctive and sometimes contentious identities.

In a narrow sense, theology is a Second Order practice that reflects on religion from within a specific community of faith and belief, particularly a Christian one. Christian theology has historically been at the heart of the Western university, and today it continues to provide the foundation for undergraduate education at many American institutions of higher learning. In these settings, the curriculum might include courses on the Bible, the history of the Christian tradition, and the beliefs and practices of the denomination with which the particular college or university is affiliated. Theologically oriented schools may also offer the opportunity to study other traditions, but they will most often be interpreted in light of Christian concerns.

For many scholars who want religious studies to have the standing of an academic discipline like all the others in the secular university (anthropology, psychology, sociology, etc.), outward theologizing (e.g., insider reflections that espouse a specifically Christian point of view) is not a valid way of approaching and representing the subject. At best, according to this view, it counts as insider data for the scholar to examine. But in current debates, theology has come to represent more than the practice of arguing for a specific perspective. The broader concern is with the theological legacy that supposedly still lurks in many contemporary approaches to religion—even those that claim to be neutral.

One tricky thing about the academic study of religion is that it grew out of both theology (a Second Order, insider phenomenon) and the "scientific" disciplines of the modern university (the Third Order). Institutionally, theology was a driving intellectual force for a very long time, so its methods have often overlapped with other disciplines. More specifically, the first religion departments in the United States (or their founders) emerged from divinity schools or departments of theology—this in just the last few decades.

So these observations have to give us pause. Perhaps the field is still in the shadow of theology. Maybe Second Order insider approaches are still embedded within the discipline. Is the study of religion just crypto-theology? For some, these suspicions point to a legacy that needs to be purged. For example, it has often been argued that religion is a *sui generis* phenomenon: that is, it is a phenomenon that is unique unto itself, of its own kind and its own kind only. So what makes it unique? For many, the answer has been simple: "religion arises to provide contact with god."[24] That in itself is a theological claim: it presupposes (a) that God exists and (b) that all religious people pursue contact with the divine, even if sometimes they do it in supposedly strange or misguided ways.

Now, scholars most often have not come right out and said that they believe that religion is about making contact with God; that would expose their view and diminish its authority in the secular university. Instead, some would argue, they use other concepts to stand in for their theology and in so doing, have produced a number of highly influential "theoretical ideas" that continue to infuse this area of inquiry: "ultimate reality," "ultimate concern," "the sacred," "the wholly other," "the transcendent," "the absolute," "thirst for being," and so on. Using ideas like these is basically interpreting religion in Second Order, reflective terms, some would argue, when what is necessary is understanding it from an academic distance, by drawing upon Third Order approaches such as philology, historical analysis, sociology, psychology, anthropology, and even the natural sciences.

You can probably see why the move to purify the study of religion of theology could lead to tension. For one thing, some strong proponents of the religious studies ethos want active theologians out of the picture. At the same time, these critics call out scholars who think they are proceeding even-handedly but actually are not: because they are using crypto-theological concepts, they are implicitly supporting or advocating for religion itself. For some, the field is always going to be tainted by its theological past. Perhaps it would be best to leave this subject matter to the members of other university disciplines, they claim. Simply maintaining something called "religious studies" or "the academic study of religion" makes an affirmation that is tacitly theological.

On the other side of this theoretical divide, scholars who draw upon ideas such as the ones presented above do not appreciate being called theologians in disguise. A term like "the sacred," for example, seems to be broad and neutral; it does not stake any particular theological claim, but instead describes a human reality. Others take a more moderate view on the role theology might play: as long as theologians rise to the standards of the Third Order of Meaning (i.e., they engage in scholarly work, make rational arguments, and allow their views to be scrutinized), why shouldn't they be allowed a place at the table? Aren't all scholars and researchers pushing a certain viewpoint? Why can't theologians do so in the study of religion, and in the broader university? As long as theologians play by the rules of academic inquiry, some would say, then they certainly shouldn't be excluded.

At the same time, some theologians respond to religious studies by simply opting out, or, interestingly enough, like their opponents on the opposite side of the spectrum, by recommending that the field be abandoned. Theology is a normative discipline (i.e., it makes a judgment about what's true or false, and right vs. wrong), and the mere description and analysis of religion hardly assists with that. Only theology can provide the answers. Indeed, if students want to know about religion they should return to their own tradition—or the one that they have been convinced to adopt—and experience its rituals, scriptures, and communities. The university should not provide them with a dim reflection of being religious second-hand. According to some, that is in fact what this field is really all about.

It would be impossible to work out all the details of this debate (let alone resolve it) here.[25] Yet it is important that you are aware of this issue before proceeding. The past still speaks, and theology will continue to have a voice in a variety of ways. Some responses to this legacy are far too extreme: abandoning the academic quest to understand religion in our day and age is unwise and borders on the irresponsible. A more moderate response will take the different Orders of Meaning seriously and, recalling the example of the Hindu student discussed above, it will be open to different voices—immediate, reflective, theological, academic, theoretical, and critical—while also listening for occasional harmonies between them.

## Conclusion

This chapter began with basic questions about what theory is and what it does, and we discovered that it is far from mysterious, abstract, or foreign; it is an everyday activity that we are all familiar with. We also discerned that theory supplements a set of operations that are vital to interpretation and understanding: definition, description, explanation, and prediction. At the same time, we had to recognize significant theoretical challenges that the field faces, namely the insider/outsider problem and its corollary, theology versus religious studies. Having thought through all of these foreground issues, you are now ready to consider some of the most prominent theories of religion that the Western intellectual tradition has produced, starting in the next chapter.

Before moving on, however, recall the way we have talked about theory: you should always be on the lookout for good "angles" or "takes," "theoretical ideas" that will give you a better look at and way through your subject matter, while constantly testing, picking and choosing, and adding your own insights. Note Clifford Geertz's position on theory, one that places you, the student, right in the middle of the whole enterprise:

> Theoretical ideas are not created wholly anew in each study . . . they are adopted from other, related studies, and, refined in the process, applied to new interpretive problems. If they cease being useful with respect to such problems, they tend to stop being used and are more or less abandoned. If they continue being useful, throwing up new understandings, they are further elaborated and go on being used.[26]

In other words, when you examine, apply, adjust, and evaluate theories in the study of religion, you are part of the process Geertz describes, part of the evolution of the field itself.

## Notes

1. *Thinking about Religion: An Historical Introduction of Theories of Religion* (Malden, MA: Blackwell Publishing, 2006), 342.
2. Matthew Day, "On the Advantage and Disadvantage of History for the Study of Religion," *Method and Theory in the Study of Religion* 20 (2008): 367.
3. Vasudha Narayanan, "Diglossic Hinduism: Liberation and Lentils," *Journal of the American Academy of Religion* 68, no. 4 (December 2000): 762.
4. William James, *The Varieties of Religious Experience: A Study in Human Nature* (New York: Penguin Books, 1987), 9.
5. Wilfred Cantwell Smith, *The Meaning and End of Religion* (Minneapolis, MN: Fortress Press, 1971), 51.

6. Walter H. Capps, *Religious Studies: The Making of a Discipline* (Minneapolis, MN: Fortress Press, 1995), 106.

7. Craig Martin, "Delimiting Religion," *Method and Theory in the Study of Religion* 21 (2009): 160.

8. See Clifford Geertz, *The Interpretation of Cultures* (New York: Basic Books, 1973), 7–8.

9. Ibid., 27.

10. Ibid., 28.

11. Robert Segal, "All Generalizations Are Bad: Postmodernism on Theories," *Journal of the American Academy of Religion* 74, no. 1 (March 2006): 157.

12. Gavin Flood, "Reflections on Tradition and Inquiry in the Study of Religions," *Journal of the American Academy of Religion* 74, no. 1 (March 2006): 49.

13. Geertz, *The Interpretation of Cultures*, 26.

14. See James D. Tabor and Eugene V. Gallagher, *Why Waco? Cults and the Battle for Religious Freedom in America* (Berkeley: University of California Press, 1995). The hypothetical scenario sketched above also draws upon David Chidester, *Salvation and Suicide: Jim Jones, the Peoples Temple, and Jonestown*, rev. ed. (Bloomington and Indianapolis: Indiana University Press, 2003).

15. See the account of this distinction in *The Insider/Outsider Problem in the Study of Religion: A Reader*, ed. Russell McCutcheon (London and New York: Cassell, 1999), 15–17.

16. Wilfred Cantwell Smith, "The Comparative Study of Religion: Whither—and Why?," in *The History of Religions: Essays in Methodology*, ed. Mircea Eliade and Joseph Kitagawa (Chicago: University of Chicago Press, 1959), 42.

17. Bruce Lincoln, "Theses on Method," in *The Insider/Outsider Problem in the Study of Religion*, 398.

18. Jonathan Z. Smith, *Imagining Religion: From Babylon to Jamestown* (Chicago and London: University of Chicago Press, 1982), xi.

19. The following framework is common in the social scientific literature; see Geertz, *The Interpretation of Cultures*, 15. This version of it draws significantly upon Sheryl L. Burkhalter, "Four Modes of Discourse: Blurred Genres in the Study of Religion," in *Beyond the Classics? Essays in Religious Studies and Liberal Education*, ed. Sheryl Burkhalter and Frank Reynolds (Atlanta: Scholars Press, 1990), 150–51; and Flood, "Reflections on Tradition and Inquiry," 55–57.

20. Burkhalter, "Four Modes of Discourse," 150.

21. Flood, "Reflections on Tradition and Inquiry," 54.

22. Burkhalter, "Four Modes of Discourse," 150–51.

23. Ibid., 151.
24. Robert A. Segal, "Theories of Religion," in *The Routledge Companion to the Study of Religion*, ed. John R. Hinnells (London and New York: Routledge, 2005), 51.
25. For a range of perspectives on this issue, see *Religious Studies, Theology, and the University: Conflicting Maps, Changing Terrain*, ed. Linell E. Cady and Delwin Brown (Albany: State University of New York Press, 2002); *Religious Studies and Theology: An Introduction*, ed. Helen K. Bond, Seth D. Kunin, and Francesca Aran Murphy (New York: New York University Press, 2003); Gavin Hyman, "The Study of Religion and the Return of Theology," *Journal of the American Academy of Religion* 72, no. 1 (2004): 195–219; *Fields of Faith: Theology and Religious Studies for the Twenty-First Century*, ed. David F. Ford, Ben Quash, and Janet Martin Soskice (Cambridge: Cambridge University Press, 2005); *Theology and Religious Studies in Higher Education: Global Perspectives*, ed. Darlene L. Bird and Simon G. Smith (London and New York: Continuum, 2009); and Christine Helmer, "Theology and the Study of Religion: A Relationship," in *The Cambridge Companion to the Study of Religion*, ed. Robert Orsi (New York: Cambridge University Press, 2012), 230–54.
26. Geertz, *Interpretation of Cultures*, 27.

# 3 Classic Theories: Part 1

In the opening chapters of this book we considered the importance of studying religion today and took methodological steps to solidify a position from which to analyze and interpret the subject matter. We also contended with some fundamental (and controversial) issues that face the student and scholar in the field.

The next two chapters build on the discussion so far and gather together a set of classic theoretical perspectives. As the quotation from Geertz at the end of the previous chapter suggested, an academic discipline gets its energy from the continual testing of compelling ideas, and if these ideas don't continue to inspire, provoke, and enlighten, then they will fade away and ultimately disappear. The theoretical frameworks that will be surveyed here have not reached that point in the academic study of religion—not even close.

The approaches investigated in this chapter move along an important axis in this field: from the individual to the social. Eminent sociologist Peter Berger has vividly described this age-old polarity and added his own spin. Human beings, he argues, come into this world incomplete; we are not guided entirely by our instincts, as is the case for animals, so society provides us with the rest of the structuring and order that we need. Thus society is generally "an area of meaning carved out of a vast mass of meaninglessness, a small clearing of lucidity in a formless, dark, always ominous jungle."[1] The individual stays in the light to the extent that his or her society is stable—and to the extent that he or she participates in its order and is simultaneously ordered by it.

These observations remind us that the status of the individual in relation to the social is a fundamental issue in studying religion. Where should we focus our attention, on individual experiences and biographies, or on the social order and the life of communities? As a sociologist, Berger places the emphasis on the latter, but as we will soon see, this is hardly the final word on the matter. His colorful metaphor adds to the interpretive mix: does religion reside in the orderly social clearing, or in more shadowy places, like the "jungle" of messy, volatile experience, both within private individuals and lurking subgroups that broader society and its institutions attempt to control and keep at bay? This chapter contains a number of responses to these provocative questions, ranging from emphasis on individual experience to social function, from religion's orderliness to the heart of its chaotic darkness.

## The Study of Religion: A Modern Phenomenon

Before moving ahead, a bit of context is necessary to explain how modern theorists were in a position to theorize about religion in the first place. People have been talking about what we now call "religion" for a very long time, long before the modern period in Europe and America, yet today we inherit a unique way of looking at it. For long stretches of human history (and this is still the case for many of our fellow human beings), it was difficult to find a place to stand outside of what we now call religion, such that studying it at a distance was even a possibility. However, the cultural and intellectual situation in Europe had shifted by the turn of the nineteenth century, opening up the prospect of systematic academic examination.

A great number of factors contributed to this transformation, too many to describe in a short book like this one. Here we can point to four major developments, however, that helped to get the academic study of religion off the ground: (1) the emergence of a clear conceptual divide between the secular and the religious; (2) a closely related emphasis on reason and thinking for oneself; (3) the development of new academic disciplines, including the scholarly study of the Bible; and (4) the renewed encounter with other cultures and religious traditions.

First and foremost, there would be no such thing as the academic study of religion—indeed, no such thing as "religion" as we have come to know it—without an assumed differentiation between the secular, nonreligious realm and the religious. This distinction was not entirely new as the modern period dawned in Europe, but in the last four centuries it has become firmly entrenched. Brutal, all-consuming wars over faith and dogma in the wake of the Reformations (among other factors) led European thinkers and political leaders to conceive of a strict divide between the public, political, economic life of a society and religion's domain. Religion was forced to retreat into its own distinct sphere—still in most instances a viable, tolerated, and protected space, but a limited one. Into the vacuum the modern, secular project flowed, with its now ubiquitous values: the nation, democracy, equality, tolerance, human rights, free markets, industrial and technological progress, and freedom from traditional prohibitions. And, as a result, "religion," as a modern phenomenon and a distinct subject of debate and inquiry, was born.

One of the more notable expressions of secularism in modern Europe was an emphasis on human reason and experience—this in opposition to accepting things on faith, or because authority figures tell us to. As far back as the seventeenth century, French thinker René Descartes (1596–1650) subjected all of his beliefs to doubt and analysis. In his *Meditations*, Descartes claimed that he would take nothing for granted and start with only what he could know for certain, which included leaving aside the data presented by the senses. The only certainty he discovered was famously *cogito ergo sum*, "I think therefore I am." Eventually Descartes was able to reconstruct a world ruled over by God and thus rely on his experience once again, but the grand gesture of subjecting everything to scrutiny resounded through the Western tradition. What should we "take on faith"? Should we in fact accept anything that we have not examined first for ourselves? For the members of the British, French, and German Enlightenment movements of the eighteenth century, religion was the cardinal example of a human institution that needed testing; it had for the most part remained unquestioned for centuries.

Following Descartes, the German philosopher Immanuel Kant (1724–1804) was one of the great champions of thinking for oneself and resisting accepted traditions. Kant urged that we "dare to be wise" (*sapere audi*), and he meant that we must exercise our rationality in all cases. So religion could only be sanctioned when it remained within the limits of reason, and particularly when it promoted rational ethical laws, such as "Do unto others as you would have done to you." As soon as it strayed into what he deemed fanaticism or superstition, Kant balked. Reason and experience are our only guides, and they can provide us with certainty in some cases, and in some cases (such as grand metaphysical questions) they cannot. But for Kant, leaping to answers based on feelings or intuitions was not an acceptable option. (It should be noted that Kant's position was relatively moderate: some of his fellow Enlighteners, for example, simply declared their atheism and argued for the abolition of religion altogether.)

Given the Enlightenment's emphasis on reason, experience, and free inquiry, it makes sense that the modern European university flowered during this period, and under its auspices, a wide range of human experience and activity was put under the microscope. Thus the Enlightenment gave birth to many of the academic disciplines that we are familiar with today, including linguistics, economics, sociology, anthropology, and the study of world literatures. It took time for the academic study of religion itself to join these ranks, but scholarly analysis of the Bible set the stage. In many ways, a major taboo against subjecting religion to academic study was broken down when historical, critical analysis of scripture became a significant scholarly project in the late eighteenth century. For example, the thought that the books of the Bible were composed in a specific time and place, within a specific historical (and very human) set of circumstances, was extremely challenging—and even more so, the developing theories that proposed that the biblical texts were composed in layers, over time, by different groups and individuals in different times, each with their own unique interests. Many rejected the idea of subjecting holy writ to this form of historical-critical analysis. It suggested, for one thing, that the Bible was not a direct, infallible product of divine revelation—or, at the very least, that the concept of revelation had to be radically reconceived. This approach also fuelled the idea that the Bible was just one profound example of human expression among many and could in fact be compared with venerable texts from other parts of the world.

And this was indeed another crucial factor that made the academic study of religion possible. Up to the modern age, Europeans had of course been encountering the rest of the world for centuries, but at the end of the 1800s a huge mass of texts, documents, and reports started to flow into the academic institutions of England, Germany, and France. This influx was the product of colonialism, the prolonged effort on the part of European nations and societies to subdue and extract wealth from the far reaches of the globe, which reached a zenith in the eighteenth, nineteenth, and early twentieth centuries.

Perhaps the most dramatic body of information came from India, which was at that time a colony within the British Empire. The longer the English remained in India, the more of its languages they learned, and the more texts they sent back to Europe. As this archive built up, it became clear that India was the home to a plethora of very ancient traditions. Discovering the depth and breadth of non-Christian religion in India gave Europe pause. Was it still possible to uphold the historical priority of biblical revelation as the original and only true source of religious sensibilities? Was European culture, which was thought to stem from an authoritative foundation in ancient Greece and Rome, truly the most profound and magnificent branch of human civilization? Or were there multiple strands of civilization, each with its own dignity, and each driven by its own unique form of religiosity? Some European intellectuals embraced the discovery of other, non-Western cultures and traditions because they seemed to represent a source of renewal; most derided these cultures and thought of them as inferior, idolatrous, and primitive. Nevertheless, the mere acknowledgment of non-Christian traditions with complex histories, intense rituals, and profound ideas all their own represented yet another challenge to European sensibilities, while also providing the starting point for cross-cultural investigation with a global span.

Contemporary religious studies scholars have subjected these factors to vigorous scrutiny and criticism. As we have already noted, there is perhaps something deeply problematic about the idea that we can (or should) draw a clean line between the religious and secular—in most cases, it just doesn't seem that simple. And for the field to be so closely aligned with secular, Enlightenment-based sensibilities has its own irony and some immediate effects. A modern, secularized understanding of religion, for example, sees it as a *segment* of society and associates it closely with the life of the individual. Within this framework, religion is something chosen by individuals as one choice among many and turns out to be a private matter, a product of personal reflection, conscience, and belief. According to some critics, this is a limiting conception that continues to afflict the field. At the same time, the link between secularism, exploitative colonialism, and the academic study of religion has received considerable attention. Does this discipline—in its most basic terminology and ground rules—contribute to a skewed understanding of the world, one that is connected with a Euro-American sense of superiority? Do the assumptions embedded in a modern, secularized study of religion cloud our understanding of the full range and experience of global traditions?

These questions remind us that the classic theoretical perspectives surveyed in the next two chapters arose in particular, rather controversial contexts—as did the academic study of religion itself.

## Religion as an Individual Experience

### Rudolf Otto

As mentioned above, German Enlightenment thinkers often attempted to defend religion as a fundamentally rational phenomenon. They argued that a lot of it simply makes sense, especially from an ethical or social standpoint. For example, "Thou shalt not kill" is a reasonable moral principle that needs no supernatural source to ratify it: it is sensible not to kill without very good reason, because we would not like to be killed ourselves. Often rituals have perfectly sensible aims as well. If we are interested in building communities that live in harmony, for example, the remembrance of a great ethical role model (such as Jesus Christ or the Buddha) might do a good job of promoting firm connections and mutual respect. According to some Enlightenment thinkers, these kinds of beliefs and practices were well worth preserving. However, there were also aspects of religion that these same figures found distracting, irrational, and even harmful, and these aspects, they claimed, should be left aside.

This rational approach to religion—and to life in general—incited reactions from Romantic movements across Europe. Romantics resisted the priority of reason and instead emphasized feeling, imagination, and nature. In Germany, Friedrich Schleiermacher (1768–1834) was an eloquent spokesman for Romanticism, and he focused his attention on rehabilitating the emotive, nonrational element within religion. Religion, Schleiermacher proposed, arises first and foremost from an experience—a feeling—that unifies the individual with the infinite (God). This feeling is expansive, overwhelming, and, as Schleiermacher himself described it, "oceanic." When we stand on the beach and look out at the expanse of the infinite ocean, or perhaps when we gaze up at the stars in the night sky, a sense of awe sometimes overcomes us. We are amazed and at the same time humbled before the grandeur of nature. This is similar to the experience at the core of religion: a feeling of absolute dependence on something tremendously powerful. Schleiermacher further noted that this experience is impossible to capture in words and ordinary expression.

Rudolf Otto (1869–1937), a German theologian and scholar of comparative religion, renewed many of Schleiermacher's views in his famous book *Das Heilige* (*The Holy*). He also clarified Schleiermacher's approach and developed categories that have been quite influential, especially in scrutinizing the individual, experiential element of religion.

*The Holy* begins with a rather shocking recommendation:

> The reader is invited to direct his mind to a moment of deeply-felt religious experience, as little as possible qualified by other forms of consciousness. Whoever cannot do this, whoever knows no such moments in his experience, is requested to read no farther; for it is not easy to discuss questions of religious psychology with one who can recollect the emotions of his adolescence, the discomforts of indigestion, or, say, social feeling, but cannot recall any intrinsically religious feelings.[2]

Here we observe a vivid example of the insider/outsider dilemma described in the previous chapter: Otto seems to be saying that one must have had a religious experience in order to understand religion. But his point is even more precise. The center of gravity, Otto argues, is not "ordinary" experiences such as family conflicts, psychosexual development, physiological needs, or social bonding. For Otto, religious experience, or an encounter with "the holy," is *sui generis* — of its own unique kind, and not reducible to other things.

"The holy," then, inspires an ineffable, nonrational experience, and encounter with this object produces "a clear overplus of meaning" that goes beyond our attempt to conceptualize it.[3] This kind of experience can only arise in response to something that is radically distinct from ordinary experience, an "unnamed Something" that Otto labels "the numinous,"[4] which first takes shape in consciousness as a feeling of absolute reliance on a creating power, as was the case for Schleiermacher. Otto's unique contribution, however, is a description of the "determinate states" of this feeling, which are captured in the Latin phrase *mysterium tremendum et fascinans* (that which is hidden, dreadful, and fascinating). The numinous (the encounter with the real presence of the "Wholly Other") inspires awe, fear, dependence, and blank wonder, but at the same time it invites fascination and attachment.

In all of these modes, the experience itself is nonrational—or perhaps more accurately "pre-rational"—but it generates rational correlates, which Otto calls "schemas." So, for example, the fearful nature of a god's holiness (experienced directly as a nonrational *feeling*) is connected with a *belief* in god's power, righteousness, and goodness; the *feeling* of numinous fascination transforms into *belief* in divine "love, mercy, pity, comfort."[5] In sum, feeling matches up with and provides the energy for concepts. Thus Otto provides a means of analyzing not only the nonrational core of religious experience, but also the way it feeds into doctrines, customs, and traditions. His own application of this theory treats examples from the Hebrew Bible, the New Testament, early Christianity, Protestantism, indigenous religions, Hinduism, and Buddhism.

You might have noticed that Otto does a lot talking about an experience that he thinks is ultimately inexpressible. This is because he had a unique purpose in mind, one that is related to his strange warning at the beginning of *The Holy*: he hoped to use approximate names and analogies "to suggest this unnamed Something to the reader . . . so that he may himself feel it."[6] In other words, Otto wanted his reader to learn about religion by having a religious experience, because otherwise it would be impossible to know what religion is all about. For many contemporary scholars, this agenda compromises Otto's entire project: scholars and teachers in an academic field have no business trying to get people experience religion; their job is to analyze, examine, and interpret it—not to promote it. Nevertheless, Otto's contribution still looms large as a strong statement on behalf of the experiential essence of religious life, and prominent scholars continue to invoke his perspective not just as a foil, but also as a positive and still valuable theoretical framework.[7]

## OTTO

"The feeling of [*mysterium tremendum*] may at times come sweeping like a gentle tide, pervading the mind with a tranquil mood of deepest worship . . . It may burst in sudden eruption up from the depths of the soul with spasms and convulsions, or lead to the strangest excitements, to intoxicated frenzy, to transport, and to ecstasy. It has its wild and demonic forms and can sink to an almost grisly horror and shuddering. It has its crude, barbaric antecedents and early manifestations, and again it may be developed into something beautiful and pure and glorious. It may become the hushed, trembling, and speechless humility of the creature in the presence of—whom or what? In the presence of that which is a *mystery* inexpressible and above all creatures."[8]

## WHAT TO LOOK FOR:

- Nonrational experiences that exceed the human ability to express them and appear to be unique to religious contexts.

- States of absolute fear and fascination within rituals, in music or art, or in connection with specific spaces and places.

- The nonrational, experiential core of rationalized religious doctrines (e.g., fear as the basis for religious laws).

### William James

William James (1842–1910), the great American philosopher and psychologist, also emphasized the experiential dimension in his landmark work *The Varieties of Religious Experience*, which "effectively launched the psychology of religion as an area of study."[9]

Like Otto, one of James's fundamental assumptions is that individual, interior, nonrational experience is more profound than general, objective, or intellectual conceptions. He states, "so long as we deal with the cosmic and the general, we deal only with the symbols of reality, but *as soon as we deal with private and personal phenomena as such, we deal with realities in the completest sense of the term*."[10] So if we wish to understand the power of something like the Bible (or any scriptural text for that matter), then we must identify the experiences that generated it, "the inner experiences of great-souled persons wrestling with the crises of their fate."[11] In the same way, the founding of any religious institution, James proposes, relies upon an original inspiration, like a direct personal communion with the divine, "so personal religion should still seem the primordial thing."[12] And the same goes for beliefs. Belief in God, for example, does not come from intellectual proofs or systematic theologies; it arises from immediate experience.

Again, like Otto, James tells us that the nonrational is a driving force in generating outward, public expression. And yet, in contrast with Otto, James was not fixated on one particular form of experience. Instead, he examined a range of religion's "varieties" and engaged in detailed comparison and description of individual cases. This attention to the particulars led to a flexible, pragmatic approach (see James's famous definition of religion, presented in the textbox below) and opened up the boundaries of his study considerably—perhaps even uncomfortably so. James was fascinated, for example, by altered or extreme states of awareness, radical moments where it seems that the unseen, supernatural world wells up at the margins of the conscious, waking life: *"if there be* higher spiritual agencies that can directly touch us, the psychological condition of their doing so might be our possession of a subconscious region which alone should yield access to them."[13]

In his pursuit of these moments, James presents a remarkable survey of melancholics saved by conversion, "normal" religious people transformed into saints through trauma and deliverance, and those on the religious fringe: mediums, supernaturalists, contemplatives, and even those considered insane by the mainstream. James's curiosity also led him to careful examination of mystical experience, which he defined by four now famous criteria:

- *Ineffability*: Mystical experiences are difficult—if not impossible—to talk about.
- *Noetic quality*: Mystical experiences seem to bestow an immediate and absolute knowledge—suddenly things that were previously confused and hidden become completely clear.
- *Transiency*: Mystical experiences come and go, passing through the consciousness like a wave that is here and gone.
- *Passivity*: Finally, mystical experiences happen *to* the subject—they are experienced as coming from somewhere else, and not directly as the result of our own actions and intentions.[14]

This analysis was a highpoint of James's inquiry: it offers a useful and productive set of descriptive categories without reducing a complex phenomenon to one thing, and one thing only.

For all of his passion, which he poured into these topics, one always has the sense that James was still a rational soul who hungered to have a profound experience himself. (He famously confesses to inhaling nitrous oxide in pursuit of this direct knowledge.) In the pages of *Varieties*, James comes off as a true American seeker who probably never quite found what he was looking for. And perhaps that is for the better: it meant that he was searching and experimenting, rather than positing absolute, watertight answers. There is something to be said for this attitude, especially when religion is the subject.

## JAMES

"Religion, therefore, as I now ask you arbitrarily to take it, shall mean for us *the feelings, acts, and experiences of individual men [and women] in their solitude, so far as they apprehend themselves to stand in relation to whatever they may consider the divine*."[15]

## WHAT TO LOOK FOR:

- The individual, nonrational experience at the core of myths, scriptures, rituals, institutions, and so on .

- Experience of external but unseen presences, "something there."

- Extraordinary states of consciousness marked by ineffability, deep insight or knowledge (a "noetic quality"), transiency, and passivity, leading to a feeling of oneness and to a breakdown of distinctions, especially between "self" and "the world."

- Religion's role in personal transformation: an interior feeling of bliss, freedom, and resolution (especially after considerable depression and suffering).

# Religion and Its Social Function

## Émile Durkheim

Moving to thinkers who emphasized the social function of religion, we now turn to Émile Durkheim (1858–1917). Durkheim was a French social scientist and one of the most important pioneers of sociology as an academic discipline. He put forth his most influential "theoretical ideas" about religion in a 1912 book called *The Elementary Forms of Religious Life*.

In the opening pages of this remarkable work, Durkheim urges his readers to clear away their preformed judgments and criticizes some commonly held views, including the notion that religion is about belief in divine beings. Instead, as a starting point, he puts forth a pair of categories that have become foundational: the *sacred* and the *profane*. This duality "is the distinctive trait of religious thought."[16] The sacred can infuse any worldly object we might imagine, and it must be treated with care because it has been deemed special, worthy, and, in most basic terms, "set apart" by the community; the profane, on the other side, is associated with the unpleasant, impure, chaotic, and oppositional.[17] The beliefs and rituals of any religious tradition, Durkheim proposes, revolve around this duality.

Durkheim adds another fundamental proposal, one goes directly against figures such as Otto and James: "religion," he argued, "is something eminently social."[18] In other words, religion cannot be rooted in an individual experience because society generates it and thus bestows it on the individual. Just as any person inherits a language he or she has not made, similarly, all religious beliefs, rituals, and representations truly belong to the collective and then manifest themselves in individual people. But without the collective, there would be no religious sensibility in the first place. In fact, Durkheim posits that the very idea of the "individual" is itself a product of society.

To flesh out these suppositions, Durkheim claims that it is necessary to go back to religion in "its most primitive and simple form."[19] A number of theorists had taken a similar *genetic* approach, leading (they thought) to the moment when religious consciousness first appeared in the ancient, primordial past (see text box, below). But Durkheim proposed a different take: he did not aim to find "the very first beginning," the moment when religion dawned on humanity. Rather, its "origin" refers to "the ever-present causes upon which the most essential forms of religious thought and practice depend."[20] In other words, the origin is always present wherever and whenever religion persists, because it is a response to—it is caused by—a universal human need.

## THREE THEORIES ABOUT THE ORIGIN OF RELIGION

- *Primordial Monotheism*: Since the eighteenth century, when detailed information about the depth and profundity of non-European, non-Judeo-Christian cultures started to emerge, some made the argument that all religions had their source in a primordial monotheistic revelation that was universal: they were all the product of an ancient, divinely inspired realization that there is one true God. Among different peoples, however, this belief eventually took on disparate, supposedly degenerate forms. In Durkheim's day, Wilhelm Schmidt (1868–1954) presented a "scientific" defense of this view, basing his argument on ethnographic information about the "Sky-God" worshiped by some Native American tribes.

- *Nature Worship*: Less theologically driven observers such as Max Müller (1823–1900) started with the material world, and with nature in particular: all religion stemmed from fear of and dependence on natural forces, which led to practices designed to appease, manipulate, and master them. Soon individual features of nature (such as the soil, animals, or storm clouds) were conceived to be divine entities, according to Müller, because of the way in which humans named them. In a sense, religion has its origins in a "disease of language," where natural forces are named in anthropomorphic terms.

- *Animism*: Other theorists such as Edward Burnett Tylor (1832–1917) suggested that religion began with the discernment of an invisible world, a world of spirits, souls, and eventually gods. He called this view animism and argued that it was the most primordial form of religion. Tylor thought that animism had its origins in two universal human experiences: (1) the sense that something invisible yet all-important leaves the body at the moment of death, and (2) the suspicion that dreams and visions make contact with a higher reality. Once the belief in a spiritual realm was established, it was only a few short steps to positing the existence of spiritual beings that stand behind nature, and behind the world as a whole.

Durkheim claimed that the "ever-present" causes of religion are most easily observed in the so-called primitive cultures. Examining ethnographic data on the aboriginal tribes of Australia, Durkheim offered his own proposal for the most elementary form: *totemism*. Totemism is based on belonging to a clan, and further, on the identification of that clan with "a determined species of material things with which it believes that it has very particular relations,"[21] mostly plants and animals. So, for example, the group might identify itself with the kangaroo, much as modern-day sports teams often take an animal as their mascot, with which fans identify. The totem is a symbol of belonging, and so it becomes sacred. The actual animal or plant is something to be protected, but it is really the symbol that is thought to protect the clan and bind it together. Myths and rituals build up around the emblem, and its representation appears everywhere, on the objects possessed by members, on their clothing, and even inscribed on their bodies. Ultimately it takes on a life of its own. Just as a nation's flag alone can compel its soldiers to fight, the symbol itself is a focus of reverence and devotion.

As a sacred object honored by generation after generation, the totem possesses *power*, a concept that is central to Durkheim's analysis. Whether that power is named *mana*, *wakan*, *orenda*, *manitou*, *tabu*, and so on among indigenous peoples, in each case we find a term for the impersonal force that stands behind the totem. Relating to this power, which imbues all things that are sacred (including human beings), is "the source of all religiosity"; even the gods, Durkheim suggests, are just "points upon which it alights."[22]

This is the moment where totemism and Durkheim's conception of religion as "eminently social" come together. The totem is, in essence, a symbol of social belonging. When totemists revere and worship their animal and organize their whole life around it, they are actually revering *themselves* as a community. As Durkheim writes, "if it [the totem] is at once the symbol of the god and of the society, is that not because the god and the society are only one?"[23] Often tribes construct rituals that are meant to instill this concept as an intense feeling of solidarity and belonging. These practices draw the individual out of himself and put him in touch with the sacred power of the totem, sometimes leading to trance-states, extreme behaviors, and "violent super-excitation."[24] Durkheim calls this experience *collective effervescence*, the experience of being swept away by the group.

To sum it all up, Durkheim's most important move is to suggest that in essence, the *functionalist* analysis of totemism applies to all religion. In every case, two functions are being fulfilled: first, religion provides a sense of social bonding and belonging and, second, it renders the community itself sacred and holy: it is made divine.

Like many of his time, Durkheim took a patronizing view of his "primi-tive" subject matter, suggesting that it was characterized by its simplicity and naivete. His theory could also be criticized for overestimating the genetic significance of totemism as a specific form, for overemphasizing the social element at the expense of the individual, or for his seeming reduction of religion to its social, bonding function. It is up to you to evaluate these potential drawbacks, especially in light of the theories of James and Otto, discussed earlier. But there is no doubt about Durkheim's significance and the power of his ideas: his social theory of religion still has significant support among contemporary scholars in the field.

## DURKHEIM

*"A religion is a unified system of beliefs and practices relative to sacred things, that is to say, things set apart and forbidden—beliefs and practices which unite into one single moral community called a Church, all those who adhere to them."*[25]

## WHAT TO LOOK FOR:

- The significance of "primitive" religions; that is, folk or indigenous traditions that do not fit into one of the major "religions of the world."

- The demarcation between the sacred and the profane, as expressed through rituals and beliefs. Practices that keep sacred and profane things separate or attempt to "manage" the power of the sacred figures (e.g., appease them or invite their help).

- Rituals that cultivate an intense feeling of bonding and belonging; symbols or emblems that have a similar effect.

- The appearance of power in objects, especially when it suggests the existence of an impersonal energy or force.

## Max Weber

Max Weber (1864–1920) was a German intellectual trained in law and economic history who eventually turned to broad investigation of social institutions. Along with Durkheim, Weber played a crucial role in the founding of modern sociology, and his scholarly attention often turned to religion.

Weber agreed with his countryman Karl Marx (discussed in the next chapter) that a basic starting point for understanding religion had to be social and economic reality. But Weber also agreed with Durkheim that religious ideas had a life of their own, independent from economic or political interests. Weber's famous attempt to bridge these two hypotheses went like this: "Not ideas, but material and ideal interests, directly govern men's conduct. Yet very frequently the 'world images' that have been created by 'ideas' have, like switchmen, determined the tracks along which action has been pushed by the dynamic of interest."[26] In other words, while the basic drive for power, status, and wealth may rule over human history, "ideas" or "worldviews" that come from religion do have the capacity to push it in a different direction.

One of Weber's most important works, *The Protestant Ethic and the Spirit of Capitalism* (published in 1904–1905), is devoted to this very theory. Here we find a remarkable story about the influence of theological concepts on the way people think about work and money. In its earliest stages, the "spirit of capitalism" was defined by those who were interested in "the earning of more and more money, combined with the strict avoidance of all spontaneous enjoyment of life."[27] Just think about Ebenezer Scrooge from Dickens's *Christmas Carol*, or Benjamin Franklin, who said, "A penny saved is a penny earned" and "Time is money." In his book, Weber wonders where this ethos came from. He argues that the inhabitants of medieval and early modern Europe generally did not follow it; they did just enough work to get by. According to Weber, the ideas promoted by seventeenth- and eighteenth-century Protestants made all the difference. The classic "Protestant work ethic," Weber argues, had its roots in a faith-based calling, a biblically sanctioned drive to work in order to display God's blessing through wealth, while simultaneously denying immediate gratification in favor of more labor, which in turn produced more wealth. Following this playbook was particularly important for those who believed in the doctrine of predestination, the idea that God had already determined who was bound for heaven and who was not: wealth, in this context, was interpreted as a sign of being among the elect.

Thus a religious system with otherworldly goals (receiving God's favor and earning a place in heaven) transmuted into the driving force behind worldly action. Such transformations occurred across the range of Protestant sects, and, as Weber demonstrates, some of the most influential early capitalists held these views—and they became very rich. This ethos spread far and wide, but eventually, as the modern era progressed, the thoughts about religious salvation detached from the spirit of capitalism. Those of us in Europe and America (and soon enough everyone else in the world) just kept working and earning, locking ourselves in what Weber called an "iron cage."[28] Capitalism had become an end in itself, its religious inspiration forgotten.

In this famous (and controversial) analysis, Weber applied one of his most important methods. His characterization of religious contributions to the "spirit of capitalism" represents an attempt to think his way into the world of interests and values in which early Protestants dwelled. To put it in Weber's terms, when applied to religion, his method of *Verstehen* (German for "understanding") required interpreting religion's "meaning" for those who adhered to it.

*Verstehen* led to another method that is central to Weber's work: he paid special attention to the "ideal types" or "carriers," highly representative adherents of a given worldview. On one level, these are public authorities such as priests, rabbis, imams, or brahmins, those who serve a community and interact with the larger world beyond: hence one of Weber's categories, *priestly* religion. But some of the most interesting figures are those who tend to take a more extraordinary approach to attaining their goals: mystics and ascetics. *Mystics*, Weber claimed, base their quest on inward experience and seek contemplative, nonrational union with the divine, leading them to flee from the world. *Ascetics* follow the same path by retiring from the world in monasteries and ashrams, but they actively strive for self-mastery, "subjecting the natural drives to a systematic patterning of life" in order to become an "instrument of god."[29] The *prophet* was another prominent type, the figure who "proclaims a religious doctrine or divine commandment" with authority, sometimes calling for a new religious sensibility, sometimes renewing the old.[30] Examples include Muhammad, the Buddha, and Jesus, who all drew upon their own inner talents to construct "a unified view of the world derived from consciously integrated and meaningful attitude toward life."[31]

It should be noted that Weber often used these categories to characterize a tradition as a whole, or a tradition at any given stage of development. That is, some religions in general seem to be particularly "priestly" in character, some "ascetic," and so on. At the same time, a tradition may have "prophetic" origins, but then it becomes dominated by some other strand. So Weber also employed these categories to account for the complexity of change and development, both as a product of outside influences, and as an interior dynamic.

One of the most interesting ways Weber talked about change is directly related to the nature of "religious virtuosos." What is the power that stands behind the most influential of these exemplary types, especially founder figures? Weber called it *charisma*, the "*extraordinary* quality of a person, regardless of whether this quality is actual, alleged, or presumed."[32] The charismatic figure possesses both obvious talents and also that *je ne sais quoi*, that special something that is at times hard to identify. Weber's most important point about charisma, however, is that it is also conferred on the leader by his or her community: the leader's power and attraction is just as much a product of the group's adoration, as it is a product of his or her own qualities.

Charisma is not only a powerful starting point for any movement or tradition, but it is also a fleeting phenomenon because it is attached to an individual. A charismatic prophet, for example, preaches his great, sometimes radical message, gathers a following interested in change and reform, and then inevitably dies. How does the community ensure that the message persists, after the prophet's departure? Weber's answer: *routinization*. It is crucial to institutionalize the radical and spontaneous eruption of the prophet, to "bottle" the charisma so the movement continues: stories are passed down, scriptures composed, rituals of remembrance enacted, sacred spaces are cordoned off, institutions set up (with leadership, official roles, etc.), and so on. You might notice that here is a tension between the presence of a spontaneous, radical, and charismatic individual and the common features of routinization (e.g., institutions, bureaucracy, routines, meetings, liturgies, etc.). However, various practices, including communal rituals, preaching, and pastoral care are often successful in recapturing the original moment, and, indeed, for a movement based on a charismatic founder to survive, Weber argued, these structures *must* be put in place.

This has been a limited sampling of what Weber had to say, but you can see that he focused on the various ways in which religion provides meaning for its followers. In fact, at the core of his analysis is the problem of suffering, the fact that terrible things happen to very good or even innocent people, and that bad people quite often get away scot-free. Weber argues that all developed religions provide a response to this challenge, in the end laying out a "stand" against a world that often seems "senseless": the religious "demand" is "that the world order in its totality is, could, and should somehow be a meaningful 'cosmos.'"[33] So religion gives adherents answers and a path to salvation, but for Weber there is a tragic edge to this seemingly positive function. As religion became more organized, complex, and bureaucratic, and as it offered more conceptual, doctrinal answers, it contributed to the "disenchantment" of the world—and in Europe and then America, it thereby set the stage for the dominance of modern, secular life and values.

It is not easy to nail down a singular theory of religion in Weber's work. He famously noted that he would not present a definition of religion until he had investigated it fully—and despite his voluminous body of work on the subject, he never thought he had investigated enough, apparently, because he left us with no concise definitional statement. But as we discovered above, in the section on William James, this open-endedness might be a virtue. Weber offers us a rich array of "theoretical ideas" to work with because he always made an exhaustive attempt to examine a worldview through and through, to see it as a living response to questions that all human beings face, and finally, to discern the way it makes sense given the interests of those who uphold it. This is what made many forms of religious expression "rational," in Weber's sense of this term: they make practical or systematic sense within the parameters of a certain problem. When the big questions are on the table, he proposed, it is indeed the case that religion—for good or ill—has often provided the most understandable response.

## WEBER

"Religious postulates can come into conflict with the 'world' from differing points of view, and the point of view involved is always of the greatest importance for the direction and for the way in which salvation will be striven for. At all times and in all places, the need for salvation . . . has resulted from the endeavor of a systematic and practical rationalization of life's realities . . . [A]ll religions have demanded a specific presupposition that the course of the world be somehow *meaningful*, at least in so far as its touches upon the interests of men [and women]. As we have seen, this claim naturally emerged first as the customary problem of unjust suffering, and hence as the postulate for a just compensation for the unequal distribution of individual happiness in the world."[34]

## WHAT TO LOOK FOR:

- The interaction between religion and other human interests and realities, particularly economics and politics.

- Examples of Weber's ideal types, carriers, and virtuosos: priests, prophets, ascetics, and mystics.

- The interplay between charisma and routinization. Who has charisma and how is it recognized? How does a tradition recapture the charisma of its founder?

- How does a religion make sense or represent a "rational" response to both "everyday" economic and political circumstances, and to basic questions of meaning, especially the problem of unwarranted suffering in the world?

## Victor Turner

In addition to sociologists like Durkheim and Weber, anthropologists have also made significant contributions to our understanding of religion. A good example is Victor Turner (1920–83), who engaged in fieldwork in Africa and then developed a highly influential theory of ritual that remains a touchstone for scholars and students in the field.

Turner based his theory on the work of an earlier anthropologist, the Belgian Arnold van Gennep (1873–1957). Van Gennep focused on "rites of passage," rituals that "accompany a passage from one situation to another or from one cosmic or social world to another."[35] Such practices mark individual transitions, such as birth, coming of age, marriage, pregnancy, embarking on or returning from a big journey, initiation, entering a holy area, or death. "Cosmic" rites of transition might also celebrate the change of seasons, the harvest, or the New Year, and "social" rituals go along with events such as the transfer of political authority or the declaration of war. To scrutinize such practices, van Gennep introduced a useful set of categories: rites of passage include a "preliminal" stage (associated with "separation"), a "liminal" stage (associated with "transition"), and a "post-liminal" stage (associated with "incorporation").[36]

What exactly do these categories describe? First it is necessary to define the term "liminal," which is central to van Gennep's theory. The adjective comes from the Latin word *limen*, which means "threshold," as in the doorway of a house. So, first, the *preliminal* stage of a rite of passage is characterized by separation from normal life. Separation is often associated with purification and preparation for undergoing the ritual. In the middle realm, the *liminal* stage itself, practices marking the transition are central, and they can be quite attention-grabbing: some tribal coming of age rituals, for example, include wearing special clothing or cutting the hair; others have more permanent effects, including tattooing, scarifying, knocking out a tooth, or even cutting off the end of a finger. Such acts radically mark the transition from one status to another (e.g., child to young adult). Finally, the *postliminal* stage ushers the participant back into society and incorporates him or her once again, but now with a new status and identity. Social celebrations that symbolize unity and reunification often mark this stage.

As van Gennep made clear, this is only a general schema. In most rituals, one of these elements is more pronounced than the others, so any given example may emphasize separation, transition, or incorporation over the others. Nevertheless, "a typical pattern always recurs: *the pattern of the rites of passage.*"[37] Victor Turner built on van Gennep's theory but then added his own ideas and findings. To cite one of Turner's favorite examples, when someone goes on a pilgrimage, symbolic gestures often mark the beginning of the holy journey, indicating separation from the normal and the everyday. And surely it is crucial to have rituals that welcome the pilgrim home again, allowing him or her to reincorporate back into the community. But what exactly happens in the heart of the journey, at the pilgrimage site itself, a "place and moment 'in and out of time'"?[38] Why does the pilgrim expect to have an encounter with the sacred there, while in the liminal phase of the journey? Why does the liminal phase have the power that it does?

First and foremost, according to Turner, rituals often open up a space where participants are "neither here nor there": they are "betwixt and between" what they were before, and what they are destined to become, as a result of the ritual process.[39] While taking part, they are also liberated from the usual social constraints because they are placed "outside or on the peripheries of everyday life."[40] So in a coming of age ritual, for example, those separated in preparation for the ceremony are neither children nor adults: they are not recognizable in terms of their status, and sometimes the community treats them that way. Being released from one's previous social identity provides an opportunity for self-reflection in the midst of the transition. But ritual, according to Turner, is not primarily about the individual, for everyone in the liminal group is in the same boat: *everyone* is "betwixt and between." The participants are stripped of identity and status, remain submissive to the leaders of the ritual, and display great homogeneity (maybe they all wear the same costume or undergo the same ritual hardships). These circumstances lead to a feeling of "intense comradeship and egalitarianism"[41]—regardless of who or what everyone was before undergoing this process.

Turner calls this feeling *communitas*, which is an essential product of liminality. Recalling Durkheim's proposals, we might call this a "bonding experience," but Turner pushes the idea further. Everyday social existence is a realm of structures and hierarchies. It's a realm of who's who, determined by an array of distinguishing characteristics, like those you might find on a census form, and, on another level, by a social scale of wealth, prestige, and power. All of this is inevitable and perhaps necessary within complex communities, but it also has a downside: "Structure is all that holds people apart, defines their differences, and constrains their actions."[42] The liminal space in ritual, in contrast, opens up a realm of *anti-structure*, for "communitas emerges where social structure is not."[43] And in this space, it is possible to experience "an essential and generic bond" that stands behind all the differences, hierarchy, and structure. A fundamental lesson is reinforced: "the high could not be high unless the low existed, and he who is high must experience what it is like to be low."[44]

While the counter-cultural, anti-structural character of liminality can confront or even threaten the normal functioning of a religious or social orthodoxy, Turner directs our attention to just how often it is in fact encouraged. Communitas sometimes springs up without much warning or planning, producing what Turner calls "existential" or "spontaneous" communitas. But quite often traditions sanction and carefully construct liminal occasions, producing "normative" communitas. Such occasions have a distinct value. For one thing, they provide a relief from the everyday: Mardi Gras, Burning Man, and Holi are examples of liminal events that have a cathartic effect for thousands each year. In a religious context, this release has deeper significance, according to Turner: it reminds the participant that adherence to a certain form of life is a matter of choice, that he or she could live otherwise, and thus remaining in the fold after the ritual renews one's commitment. In addition, as we have seen, the ritual process re-forges a sense of common social identity, a feeling of "human-kindness" and solidarity that is often missing in everyday life. Finally, it also opens a space for creativity, innovation, and change. Because rituals open up an indeterminate, anti-structural realm of experience, they are full of potential for looking at the world in a dramatically different way. Freed from everyday "clichés," social status, and "role playing," those in the limen have a chance to think things anew[45] and bring new insights back into the community to which they belong. One might go so far as to say that all great developments in human consciousness arise from a liminal space. Figures such as Jesus and the Buddha were certainly "betwixt and between," and they called for communitas and anti-structure in the midst of rigid, hierarchical societies.

This state is so prized that a religion (and sometimes whole societies) will support the existence of permanent, liminal institutions. Turner cites the example of monks and nuns who establish egalitarian communities and escape the structures of social life. Such groups have historically provided release from the rules and norms that govern the majority, while also reminding traditions about their core values. In modern society, Turner suggests, nonreligious "liminoid" groups have served a similar function. Counter-cultural artists, for example, who have at times chosen a life of relative poverty and communal living, have provoked and made us think. At the same time, in modern, secularized societies, religion itself becomes something of a liminal space that provides anti-structure and communitas in a bureaucratic and compartmentalized world.

Turner generated his theory of the ritual process in the late 1960s, and it shows. He often associated liminality and communitas with "hippies" and "beats," "who 'opt out' of the status-bound social order"[46] in order to have "a transformative experience that goes to the root of each person's being and finds in that root something profoundly communal and shared."[47] To this extent, Turner's theory is somewhat romantic. For him, rituals and counter-cultures have the tendency to reinforce our common humanity, and not our divisions. This view seems a bit naïve—you can be the judge. Nevertheless, in his account of the liminal stage of ritual activity, Turner provides us with a conceptual framework that attempts to explain the sacred core of religious life, which resides in practices and communities that disrupt the normal patterns and structures of existence. This is where the higher realities speak, according to this highly influential anthropologist and his many scholarly followers.

## TURNER

"The great historical religions have, in the course of time, learned how to incorporate enclaves of communitas within their institutionalized structures—just as tribal religions do with their *rites de passage*—and to oxygenate, so to speak, the 'mystical body' by making provisions for those ardent souls who wish to live in communitas and poverty all their lives. Just as in a ritual of any complexity there are phases of separation from and reaggregation to the domain of the social structure . . . and a liminal phase representing an interim of communitas . . . so does a great religion or church contain many organizational and liturgical sectors which . . . maintain in a central position a sanctuary of unqualified communitas."[48]

## WHAT TO LOOK FOR:

- Ritual in its many forms, especially "rites of passage": birth, coming of age, marriage, initiation, funerals, and so on.

- The structure of specific rituals: separation, liminality, and reincorporation or reaggregation.

- The power of liminality: communitas and anti-structure at the heart of ritual.

- Perennial liminal institutions that have developed within a religious tradition.

- Pilgrimage as a particularly vivid example of the theory.

## Clifford Geertz

In the previous chapter you already encountered a famous strategy proposed by another American anthropologist, Clifford Geertz (1926–2006), namely, "thick description." Geertz spelled out the theory behind this practice in a well-known 1966 essay titled "Religion as a Cultural System." In this essay, Geertz tells us that religion is an aspect of culture, and as such, it is part of a "historical transmitted pattern of meanings embodied in symbols. . .by means of which men communicate, perpetuate, and develop their knowledge about and attitudes toward life."[49] But what is unique to religion? How specifically does it fit into the bigger puzzle of cultural meaning? To answer these questions, Geertz offered a well-known definition (see the textbox below), which we now proceed to unpack.

First, according to Geertz, religion is "*a system of symbols*." Symbols are "tangible" and "perceptible" things that stand in for abstractions such as "ideas, attitudes, judgments, longings, or beliefs."[50] Examples include everything from the written number "6" to the cross in Christianity. But Geertz also says that a religion is a "*system*," so it is a grouping of symbols that hang together in a stable set of relationships, like a language. Because they include these kinds of complex networks of meaning, religious traditions provide a comprehensive map of the world and how to live in it. Geertz captures this capacity of a "system" by saying that it provides both "models of" and "models for." "Models of" describe or give a representation of the world, like a model of an atom or a map, and "models for" are like a blueprint for a building that has not yet been constructed: they tell us how to do it. As a "*system of symbols*," religion provides both a *model of* the world we inhabit (it describes it) and a *model for* our activity in the world (it recommends how to shape it).

Geertz also emphasizes the unique way a religious symbol system takes root: it produces "*powerful, pervasive, and long-lasting moods and motivations*."[51] A religion cultivates a mind-set that keeps its participants invested. Through practice, upbringing, and ritual, it cultivates "*motivations*," different directions in character such as "moral circumspection" or "dispassionate tranquillity," and "*moods*," temporary mental states that are attached to the symbols of the religious system.[52] In these ideas Geertz attempts to bring together the impersonal, inherited realm (no individual Christian "thinks up" a symbol like the cross: it is a given from the beginning) and the experience of the individual practitioner.

Why does a seemingly impersonal system of symbols, which after all are merely objects that stand in for abstractions, have the power to evoke powerful moods and motivations? Borrowing from Weber, Geertz claims that a coherent religious system provides a sense of order in a world that often threatens us with meaninglessness. A religion "must . . . affirm something," "some transcendent truths" that can account for seeming anomalies and absurdities in life.[53] Again, like Weber, the most serious existential challenge that we face is the problem of seemingly unwarranted suffering, where bad things happen to good people and vice versa. But Geertz adds his own twist. The task of a religious system of meaning, he says, is not to resolve the problem or even to avoid suffering. Rather, as an ordered system of reliable ideas about the world that also evokes "*moods and motivations*," a religion helps its followers "make of physical pain, personal loss, worldly defeat, or the helpless contemplation of others' agony something bearable, supportable—something, as we say, sufferable."[54] In fact, in exploring the gap between the ways things are and the way they ought to be, religions may actually celebrate it—as long as there are powerful symbols that can come to the rescue and at least account for the elusive nature of the answers to our big questions.

In the final part of his definition, Geertz urges us to think about why religious people might come to believe in all of this stuff in the first place. Where does the "*aura of factuality*" come from? Why does it seem true for so many? This authority can come from many places, including long-standing traditions, individual experience, charismatic leaders, or revealed scriptures, but everything, Geertz claims, can be boiled down to a simple formula: "he who would know must first believe."[55] And belief is cultivated within ritual, "[f]or it is in ritual . . . that this conviction that religious conceptions are veridical [true] and that religious directives are sound is somehow generated."[56] Echoing figures such as Durkheim and Turner, in ritual everything meets up: the symbols—the "models of" the world and "models for" life—are represented, the "*moods and motivations*" are evoked, and a sense of order and meaning is cultivated.

You can probably see how "thick" a description of any given religious phenomena would have to be if it were to take Geertz's theory as a starting point. Complex symbol systems and their relation to other symbol systems need our attention, as do the "*moods and motivations*" of individual practitioners. The Weberian challenge, the "problem of meaning," also calls out for examination, and finally, if that's not enough, we have to learn how to read rituals in all their meaning and significance for communities and practitioners. Obviously Geertz's theory is not for the shy; it puts the ball in our court and challenges us to delve into religion in all its complexity. That is surely its greatest merit: there's no shortage of compelling "theoretical ideas" here that usher us into the subject matter, which (as Geertz reminds us) is fascinating precisely because it is so intricate.

## GEERTZ

"*[A] religion is: (1) a system of symbols which acts to (2) establish powerful, pervasive, and long-lasting moods and motivations in men by (3) formulating conception of a general order of existence and (4) clothing these conceptions with such an aura of factuality that (5) the moods and motivations seem uniquely realistic.*"[57]

## WHAT TO LOOK FOR:

- Religious symbols that form a coordinated, interlocking system of meaning for adherents.

- The moods and motivations a religion promotes, and how it cultivates them.

- A religion's response to the "Problem of Meaning." How does it teach the believer "how to suffer"? Does it identify the line between the way the world is as opposed to what it ought to be? How does it contend with that dilemma?

- Production of an "aura of factuality" in a community or tradition, especially by means of ritual.

## Conclusion: Welcome to the Jungle

So where does religion essentially reside, in the experience of the individual, or in the structures of society? And further, does it open up a bright, ordered clearing, or does it come from out there, in the shadowy jungle of the nonrational? On one side, we have to admit that religion would be nothing without individuals to experience it (and experience it deeply and passionately); on the other, there's no religion without communities that come together and build it—in fact, there may be no heightened individual experience without some kind of group to foment it. Hence the dilemma: is our subject discovered primarily within the "feelings, acts, and experiences of individual[s] . . . in their solitude," as James would have it, or is it "eminently social," as Durkheim would claim? To take the issue one step further, this chapter has also discussed a number of theorists who align the essence of religion with the nonrational: James and Otto present clear examples of this move. Other figures, such as Durkheim and Weber, see religion, society, and rational order as closely linked.

Of course, such issues are rarely either/or, and all of the theorists we have discussed so far recognized that the opposites must somehow come together: individuals must experience what religion has to offer, communities must come together for it to persist; shadows creep into the clearing, just as the campfire can penetrate the jungle. But in the task of interpretation, it is always a question of emphasis: in any given case, which perspective is more instructive? The ideas you have studied so far are ready for your testing and application. But the range of possibilities only increases in the next chapter.

## Notes

1. Peter L. Berger, *The Sacred Canopy: Elements of a Sociological Theory of Religion* (New York: Doubleday, 1967), 23.
2. Rudolf Otto, *The Idea of the Holy*, trans. John W. Harvey (London, Oxford, and New York: Oxford University Press, 1958), 8.
3. Ibid., 5.
4. Ibid., 7.
5. Ibid., 31.
6. Ibid., 6.
7. See Robert A. Orsi, "The Problem of the Holy," in *The Cambridge Companion to Religious Studies*, ed. Robert A. Orsi (New York: Cambridge University Press, 2012), 84–105.
8. Ibid., 12–13.
9. Ann Taves, "William James Revisited: Rereading *The Varieties of Religious Experience* in Transatlantic Perspective," *Zygon* 44, no. 2 (June 2009): 416.
10. William James, *The Varieties of Religious Experience: A Study in Human Nature* (New York: Penguin Books, 1987), 498.
11. Ibid., 5.
12. Ibid., 30.
13. Ibid., 242.
14. Ibid., 380–82.
15. Ibid., 31.
16. Émile Durkheim, *The Elementary Forms of Religious Life*, trans. Joseph Ward Swain (New York: The Free Press, 1965), 52.
17. See William Paden, "Reappraising Durkheim for the Study and Teaching of Religion," in *The Oxford Handbook of the Sociology of Religion*, ed. Peter B. Clarke (Oxford: Oxford University Press, 2011), 37.
18. Ibid., 22.
19. Ibid., 15.
20. Ibid., 20.
21. Ibid., 123.
22. Ibid., 229.
23. Ibid., 236.
24. Ibid., 248.
25. Ibid., 62.

26. Max Weber, *From Max Weber: Essays in Sociology*, trans. H. H. Gerth and C. Wright Mills (New York: Oxford University Press, 1958), 280.

27. Max Weber, *The Protestant Ethic and the Spirit of Capitalism*, trans. Talcott Parsons (New York: Charles Scribner's Sons, 1958), 53.

28. Ibid., 181.

29. Max Weber, *The Sociology of Religion*, trans. Ephraim Fischoff (Boston, MA: Beacon Press, 1991), 164.

30. Ibid., 46.

31. Ibid., 59.

32. Weber, *From Max Weber*, 295.

33. Ibid., 281.

34. Ibid., 353.

35. Arnold van Gennep, *The Rites of Passage*, trans. Monika B. Vizedom and Gabrielle L. Caffee (Chicago: University of Chicago Press, 1960), 10.

36. Ibid., 11.

37. Ibid., 191.

38. Ibid., 197.

39. Victor Turner, *The Ritual Process: Structure and Anti-Structure* (Ithaca, NY: Cornell University Press, 1989), 95.

40. Victor Turner, *Dramas, Fields, and Metaphors* (Ithaca, NY: Cornell University Press, 1974), 47.

41. Turner, *The Ritual Process*, 95.

42. Turner, *Dramas, Fields, and Metaphors*, 47.

43. Turner, *The Ritual Process*, 126.

44. Ibid., 97.

45. Ibid., 128.

46. Ibid., 112.

47. Ibid., 138.

48. Ibid., 267.

49. Clifford Geertz, *The Interpretation of Cultures* (New York: Basic Books, 1973), 89.

50. Ibid., 91.

51. Ibid., 94.

52. Ibid., 96–97.

53. Ibid., 98–99.

54. Ibid., 104.

55. Ibid., 110.

56. Ibid., 112.

57. Ibid., 90.

# 4 Classic Theories: Part 2

You might remember from Chapter 2 that the English word "theory" comes from an ancient Greek term, *theoria*. The great philosopher Plato was one of the first thinkers to breathe life into this notion. In one of his most influential works, *The Republic*, Plato offers a demonstration of theoretical vision in his famous "Allegory of the Cave." This story provides us with a blueprint for this chapter, which discusses a wide range of perspectives—from intense criticism of religion on one side, to affirmation of it on the other.

At a certain point in *The Republic*, Plato asks us to imagine a group of human beings trapped in a dark cave. Chains bind them to the floor and prevent them from looking at anything besides the back wall. Behind them and at some distance, an intense bonfire burns, and between these people and the fire there is a partition, along which attendants carry various objects that cast shadows. These images projected on the back wall of the cave are the only things that the chained prisoners can see, the only reality that they know.

After establishing this scenario, Plato encourages us to consider what would happen if one of these prisoners broke free, turned, saw the puppet show that cast the shadows, and then made his or her way out of the cave. At first the sunlight would be blinding, and the escapee would be disoriented. But then he or she would perceive the beautiful world outside. What if this liberated individual then returned, to educate former comrades about the magical place beyond? Without a doubt, they would call this person crazy, drive him or her away, and maybe even try to inflict harm—because everything that they thought they knew was being challenged.

In the ancient Greek sense of the term, theory is "deep seeing," or seeing what really is the case. So the rebel in Plato's story has gained an understanding of the reality behind the shadowy images and has also seen something even more dramatic: an entirely different, more mean-ingful world—a realm, according to Platonic philosophy, of eternal and unchanging truths that makes everything else pale in comparison. Then this "theorist" has tried to share this vision with everyone else, but with little prospect for success.

In connection with the study of religion, this episode raises an inter-esting question: where does the truth reside? For some, religion is the greatest of illusions, a force that creates the shadowy images that keep people entranced, distracted, and deluded. So a proper *theory* of reli-gion, according to these critics, should in fact free us from it. For others, it is our everyday world that puts us under the spell of superficial, tran-sitory, material things. And so *theory* should break these attachments and lead us out of the cave, into the light of the truth at the core of religiosity.

In the present context, it is not our job to come to an ultimate conclusion about these matters: that task has been traditionally left up to philosophers and theologians, not students of the academic study of religion. But the fact is, theorists working along this spec-trum—from vigorous attack to committed caretaking—all have something to offer to a more even-handed analysis. Even the harsh-est critics have contributed constructive, widely applicable insights, and a theologian's commitment to a particular faith does not neces-sarily invalidate his or her general approach to religion. As always, it is up to you to evaluate these ideas, to think about and anticipate which ones might assist in interpreting and understanding the data most effectively.

Is religion inside of the cave or out? That's hard to answer, but whatever else *theoria* might be, Plato tells us that it frees the mind and improves our ability to see what's really the case. All the figures discussed below, as diverse as they are, would likely agree on this basic motive.

## Religion as Illusion

As the previous chapter indicated, the Enlightenment period had a tremendous impact on the way we look at religion. You will recall that the philosopher Immanuel Kant laid down the challenge: "Dare to be wise." Kant was calling for humanity to grow up. For centuries, according to him, unquestioned beliefs and superstitions had dominated, but the time had come for human beings to think for themselves. Religion needed to be put on trial in the court of reason.

One of the most significant trends in the modern critique of religion emerged in German thought after Kant. G. W. F. Hegel (1770–1831), for example, took Kant's "dare to be wise" to the extreme: in one of his works, he claimed to be thinking the thought of God before creation! God's thought, or the "mind" or "spirit" (*Geist*) behind everything, provided the conceptual playbook for the way the world has unfolded, according to Hegel. Strangely enough, for *Geist* to realize its plans, and for it to see and know itself, it had to try to view itself from the outside, to go outside itself and make itself concrete and particular, not just abstract and universal. It did just that in the material world and in humanity in particular. But at the same time *Geist* became alienated from itself. Humanity is that alienated portion, a little bit of genuine self-knowledge, constantly running up against a world that does not seem to make sense at all, blocking it from coming home. As Hegel attempted to show, however, throughout history the human intellect had gradually made progress in politics, the arts, philosophy, and, of course, in religion. Finally, in his day and age, Hegel claimed that *Geist* had arrived at itself again, largely because a human mind (Hegel's) had understood it.

While this system scaled the heights of human reason, some critics isolated its theological undertones: *Geist*, which Hegel associated with the mind of God, was indeed at its center. Ludwig Feuerbach (1804–72) drew heavily on Hegel, but as a staunch humanist, he reversed his scheme. In *The Essence of Christianity* (1841), Feuerbach argued that Hegel got it all wrong. It's not the divine "mind" that is alienated from itself in making humans; rather, the human "mind" is alienated from itself by making God. This process begins with humans imagining the infinite, which then takes on a life of its own: we allow ourselves to forget that we were the ones who conceived of the idea of the infinite in the first place. Feuerbach asserts that it is in us, as human beings, in our potential, not "out there" as the essential quality of an object (like God). But once the infinitely powerful object is set up, we give everything over to it; we project positive human qualities on it and then renounce those qualities in ourselves (e.g., love, mercy, justice, power, etc.). We say, "It's all in God's hands," and as a consequence, this projected image causes human beings to swear off what is best and most profound in themselves. In response, Feuerbach recommended overcoming this illusion by recognizing that God and religion are of our own making.

Here you should take note of two concepts that are central to the modern critique of religion: *alienation* and *projection*. Modifying Hegel, Feuerbach proposed that religious belief alienates human beings from themselves, from their own true nature and potential. Illusions that we ourselves have constructed and projected enthral us, and Feuerbach called for them to be dispelled. During the next century, a number of thinkers, including Karl Marx and Sigmund Freud, took this form of criticism to its full, radical extent.

## Karl Marx

Karl Marx (1818–83) is of course famous for his opposition to capitalism and his formulation of communism, but he also generated a highly influential theory of religion, one that has resonated in sociology and religious studies up to the present day.

Marx rejected the highly abstract philosophy of his era (like Hegel's) and promoted a materialist perspective that was designed to have practical implications for the human condition. Turning away from the "rule of thoughts,"[1] Marx focused on "real individuals, their activity and the material conditions under which they live."[2] Humans are finite, biological entities who have a remarkable ability to produce things and refashion nature. So the truth of human existence is on the ground, in the organization of labor, goods, and exchange. The point of uncovering this truth, according to Marx, is to make life better: "The philosophers have only *interpreted* the world. . .the point is to *change* it."[3]

So if human nature is essentially biological and economic, where do our complicated human institutions come from? What about our grand political, legal, moral, and philosophical ideals? Marx's answer: from the "material life-process" itself. History is really the story of people putting food on the table, making sure they have a roof over their heads, and trying to reproduce both themselves and their wealth. Abstractions ("ideology" in Marx's terms) are a product of those arrangements. Morality, religion, politics, and philosophy mirror the reality of history, the material conditions of our survival.

Because history is all about these material conditions, it is also a story of inequality and conflict. From the earliest moments of social interaction, one individual or group commands the work of others, so there is a "division of labor." Each person is assigned a particular job—but whoever is in charge reaps most of the benefits. The most basic distinction, therefore, is the one between the property owners and the propertyless laborers. As this distinction becomes more differentiated, it becomes the origin of classes, such as aristocrats, the middle class, and workers. Class struggle is the engine of history for Marx, and along the way, it generates more abstract forms of culture.

To this extent, Marx agreed with Feuerbach that humans invented religion, and yet he identified its origins more concretely. As a general rule, Marx asserted that the situation for the vast majority of people throughout history had been miserable. Culminating in the modern, capitalist system, the owners of the means of production (the property, the labor, the factories, etc.) made more and more profit simply because they owned. The huge divide between the haves and the have-nots led to intense physical hardship for the masses. It also generated various forms of psychological alienation. For one thing, the buying and selling of workers' effort dehumanized them as they fulfilled economic roles that had largely been forced upon them. In addition, modern industrial laborers performed one repetitive action over and over again on an assembly line and never had the satisfaction of seeing the end result. Moreover, the inevitable competition between workers led to the unraveling of social bonds, except for those that served the interest of the owner.

From Marx's analytical perspective, the exploitation of the masses was obvious, and yet relatively few could see it. Why? The answer: ideology, and its worst form, religion. Like every abstract form of consciousness,

Marx proposed, religion expresses the underlying material conditions that are dominant in any given period, but its essential function is to keep people from thinking about the reality of their situation. Thus "the criticism of religion is the premise of all criticism"; religion is the essence of the illusions that keep human beings in bondage and servitude because it discourages analysis and critique in general. So dispelling this illusion is the first step in dispelling them all.[4]

This said, Marx was not *entirely* dismissive of religion because he claimed to have uncovered its origins. He acknowledged that it expresses the impoverishment, suffering, exploitation, and alienation of the masses throughout history. Hence "[r]eligion is the sigh of the oppressed creature, the sentiment of a heartless world, and the soul of soulless conditions. It is the *opium* of the people."[5] To this extent, Marx found the persistence of religious beliefs and practices understandable. For someone who is paid next to nothing to work under terrible conditions, reverence for the nobility of silent suffering, belief in an eternal soul that is different from the body, and hope for eternal life in a better world after this one are reasonable responses. While they are in fact false, these commitments numb the pain of a profoundly difficult life.

And yet, according to Marx, these ideologies provide only a temporary fix that ultimately blinds the exploited laborer and serves interests of those in charge: "The ideas of the ruling class are in every epoch the ruling ideas."[6] This means that religion expresses "the sigh of the oppressed," but at the same time it manipulates and controls. For example, from a Marxian perspective, it's good for the capitalist factory-owner if his workers adhere to basic Christian principles. Be humble. Follow the example of the suffering Christ. Purify yourself through work. Avoid wealth and material things. Suppress the needs and desires of the body. Think about your treasure laid up in heaven, not about this world. And so on. Only by shedding such ideological illusions could the workers see the reality of their situation and take action to improve it.

Despite his antipathy toward religion, it could be said that Marx had his own messianic, utopian vision of heaven on earth. He predicted that the division between the haves and the have-nots would reach a breaking point, and as a result, the workers would overthrow their masters in a massive global revolution and then institute a propertyless, classless society. This vision was highly idealistic, but, indeed, Marx's purpose was not to interpret the world but to change it. Marx's critical analysis was designed to serve this agenda, and his theory does tend toward reductionism by suggesting that religion is solely an illusory product of economic circumstances—and that it is really nothing of substance unto itself. Nevertheless, he was also a precursor for more moderate and nuanced theories. Marx thought that any abstract form of human consciousness is itself a social product, which reminds us that we must see even the most elusive or esoteric religious forms in the context of concrete historical, social, and economic circumstances. As the discussion of figures such as Durkheim and Weber in the previous chapter has shown, applying this insight doesn't have to make us as antagonistic toward the subject matter as Marx himself was. Both these figures were clearly influenced by Marx, and they developed theories that were designed to understand and explain their object of study, not to criticize and undermine it.

## MARX

"The basis of irreligious criticism is this: *man makes religion*; religion does not make man . . . It is *the fantastic realization* of the human being inasmuch as the human being possesses no true reality . . . Religious suffering is at the same time an expression of real suffering and a protest against real suffering. Religion is the sigh of the oppressed creature, the sentiment of a heartless world, and the soul of soulless conditions. It is the *opium* of the people."[7]

## WHAT TO LOOK FOR:

- The material and economic conditions under which people live, and the effect of these conditions on religious belief and practice. Religion and work, class, money, property, and politics.

- Does participation in religion distract people from their economic circumstances? Does it serve to manipulate or cloud the minds of its adherents? Is it the "opium of the people"?

- The situation of both the oppressed and the ruling elite: Where does religion serve the interests of both these groups?

- Religion as a commodity: the marketing and selling of religious objects, experiences, membership, and so on.

# Sigmund Freud

Like Marx, Sigmund Freud has become a household name. His ideas, like "the ego," "the unconscious," and "the talking cure" (therapy), are now part of our everyday vocabulary. And also like Marx, Freud presented a theory of religion that ultimately aimed to expose it as a massive, harmful fantasy. The classic formulation of this theory appeared in the 1927 work, *The Future of an Illusion*.

Freud is most famous for his contributions to the psychology of the individual. For example, thanks to *psychoanalysis*, the general name for Freud's approach, we now think of childhood as formative, particularly in structuring the libidinal drive, the in-born desire for pleasure and satisfaction. In one of Freud's classic accounts of childhood development, the mother is the first love-object for the child because she is the first to offer nourishment and comfort. But soon enough, the father steps in. This intervention produces ambivalence: the child fears the father as a distant authority figure and perhaps even resents him for interfering with the intimate connection with the mother, but at the same time the child reveres the father and wants to share in his power. So, from the very beginning, we are embroiled in a complex set of relationships, within which we grow and seek satisfaction.

Most often, a lot is suppressed in the unfolding of this drama, which Freud called "the Oedipus complex." To a certain extent this is healthy and appropriate: to become mature human beings, we need to be able to control our desires and bodily needs. Yet, according to Freud, depending on how these desires and needs are handled by the parents (if they are subjected to intense scrutiny, shame, and/or punishment, for example), they become diverted or buried—and then they transform into the subconscious forces behind unhealthy behaviors, moods, and emotions in adulthood. These subterranean forces, set in motion in childhood, often beyond the reach of conscious memory, are not always easy to acknowledge or understand. Instead, they show up, garbled by the transition from the unconscious to the conscious mind, in dreams, in slips of the tongue, and in misdirected obsessions and attachments. If the submerged "baggage" is overwhelmingly difficult and traumatic, harmful symptoms appear that keep the individual from living a happy life. But fortunately Freud devised a cure: talking to an analyst (a therapist), who serves as a guide to unraveling the problem. The goal of psychoanalysis is to encourage the "rational operation of the intellect" to replace "the effects of repression"[8] so the patient can live a life free of neurosis and misery.

In *Future of an Illusion*, Freud generalizes this theory and applies it to "civilization." Society grows like an individual, and for it to function, basic instincts need to be kept in check or properly channeled. But the problem is, according to Freud, that people have the instincts regardless—there's no way to eliminate our basic desire for sex, food, pleasure, satisfaction, and mastery. So what do we do? The answer: we must receive something from society in return for suppressing our true desires. No one really likes to sacrifice instant gratification in favor of hard work, for example, but society encourages this behavior and bestows "mental assets" as compensation. One might have to work twelve-hour days to make ends meet, but one can always take pride in being "the salt of the earth," possessing a strong "work ethic," or maybe even better yet, being a citizen of a powerful nation, who has a "share in the task of ruling other nations and dictating their laws."[9] Like Marx, Freud believed that such abstractions both expressed and masked real conditions of human existence. But Freud emphasized the libidinal part of our nature, which perhaps explains the appeal of such "mental assets": we want what we want, so for an idea to distract us from our desires, it must be intensely satisfying as compensation.

But the cultural ideals of our civilization, like being a good citizen, a good wife or husband, a solid worker, proud soldier, and so on can only do so much. When confronted with the harsh realities of our existence, particularly the overwhelming force of nature and the inevitability of degeneration and death, "the work of civilization" is not quite enough.[10] This existential anxiety requires something even more soothing: the imagined presence of the gods. Freud argues that the gods are a collective representation of our individual experience. Deep down, he suggests, each of us knows the experience of fear and dependence because of our helplessness as infants and children. Our parents (in most instances) took care of our material and emotional needs—these needs could not have been met without them. When it comes to cosmic anxieties, however, we need BIG parents, and so we engage in an act of projection and then call out to divine presences for help. We imagine that they care for us in the face of death, disaster, and chaos, so they must be ultimately benevolent and quite powerful. But with divine power also comes a feeling of intimidation and fear. Something with the ability to sustain us in the face of cosmic meaninglessness must be kind and compassionate, but also a little overwhelming, scary, and even ferocious.

The projection of individual experience into a collective representation is most clear in Western monotheism, according to Freud: the belief in the one true God—the Father God. The imaging of this God as a frightening but simultaneously benevolent father is a tip-off to Freud that this belief is indeed a projection. If religion's function is to stave off fear, weakness, and frailty, the construction of a powerful father-figure who controls nature and promises the overcoming of death makes a great deal of sense, as does the desire of the religious person to be a good child in the eyes of the Father God, in order to become worthy of his love. These religious ideas—and others like them—provide a powerful fulfillment of our wish to be free from helplessness and anxiety. They also provide a satisfying compensation for whatever has gone wrong in our lives. Even if everything has fallen apart, the God is still there, with the promise of a better life after this one, offering a comforting, eternal embrace.

Much of Freud's critique relies on a basic presupposition: religious beliefs cannot be empirically proven, and thus they are irrational. No one can prove, for example, that there is an immortal soul or a God—people believe in such things because they need and want to. Therefore, religion is illusory, and "[n]othing blurs the distinction between normal and pathological so much as religion."[11] So what is to be done about it? Freud acknowledged that "[r]eligion has clearly performed great services for human civilization. It has contributed much towards the taming of the asocial instincts."[12] But in keeping with his overarching theory, Freud notes that the continuing search for and obsession with imagined substitute parent figures—not to mention sexual prudery, which is a common feature of religious teachings—are signs of someone who "is destined to remain a child for ever, [who] can never do without protection against strange superior powers."[13] Just like the individual, the civilization that maintains an illusory basis for its cultural ideals and moral precepts needs therapy—the rational analysis of the scientific observer—in order to grow up and out of its childishness.

It should be noted that *Future of an Illusion* does not exhaust Freud's reflections on religion. He also commented extensively on totemism, fetishism, and monotheistic traditions. In addition, he was fascinated by ritual, and in a 1907 essay titled "Obsessive Actions and Religious Practices," Freud explored the connections between what we would now call obsessive-compulsive behavior and religious rituals. While they are not the same, Freud suggested that both are the expression of repressed desires, often of a sexual nature. More importantly, Freud drew attention to the way in which ritual tends to transform seemingly meaningless gestures or otherwise insignificant details into matters of great significance. Religion in this sense is a focusing lens, diverting attention from basic instincts that have been deemed socially or psychologically unacceptable to symbolic, ritualized attachments.

Thus we can see one way in which Freud's theoretical ideas, while originally designed to undermine religion, still might contribute to a more balanced approach. Freud used a metaphor that is reminiscent of Marx's "opium of the people": religion is the "sweet—or bitter-sweet—poison."[14] Nevertheless, "Freud was not only a *critic* of religion, he was also an *analyst* of religion."[15] Along with figures such as William James (discussed in the previous chapter), he opened a whole new vista by linking individual psychology—particularly the psychology of human desire—with religious commitments. Perhaps what we are talking about here is indeed the remarkable transformation of the small, the intimate, and the erotic into a grand projection on a very large screen.

## FREUD

"Religion would thus be the universal obsessional neurosis of humanity; like the obsessional neurosis of children, it arose out of the Oedipus complex, out of the relation to the father. If this view is right, it is to be supposed that a turning-away from religion is bound to occur with the fatal inevitability of a process of growth, and that we find ourselves at this very juncture in the middle of that phase of development."[16]

## WHAT TO LOOK FOR:

- The expression of sexual desire and physiological satisfaction in religious contexts.

- The mirroring of family dynamics in religious symbols and doctrines.

- The connection between individual, psychological history and religious commitment: religion as "wish-fulfillment."

- Obsession in religious contexts, either with doctrines or ritual objects and activities.

# Phenomenology of Religion: Symbols, Patterns, and Dimensions

## Carl Jung

To make the transition between psychoanalysis and the phenomenological approach—and also to move from explicitly critical views of religion to neutral, or even affirmative perspectives—we turn to Carl Jung (1875–1961). Jung was a collaborator with Freud until the two parted ways because of disagreements about the nature of psychoanalysis. Jung also resisted Freud's criticism of religion and invoked phenomenological method in an attempt to present a more sympathetic account.

We have already discussed phenomenological method in earlier chapters. You will recall that this approach requires that we bracket our prior beliefs and attitudes before studying something. This supposedly leaves us open to the phenomena as they truly appear, allowing us to observe and describe them without prejudice. In *Psychology and Religion* (1937), Jung rejected the Freudian agenda and claimed that his approach is "exclusively phenomenological, that is, it is concerned with occurrences, events, experiences, in a word, with facts. Its truth is a fact and not a judgment."[17] Jung goes on to use the virgin birth of Jesus as an example. The point for a psychologist is not to determine whether it really happened or not; instead, the mere fact that people possess the belief is all that matters. You will notice that this perspective differs radically from both Marx and Freud, whose investigations were designed to expose such views as illusory.

But Jung did agree with Freud on many points, including the importance of the unconscious. Freud had already shown that the unconscious was a deep well of desires that had often been suppressed. Then, at some later point, they returned, and Freud mined obsessions, slips, dreams, and associations to discern what the unconscious was trying to say. Symbols, therefore, had to be at the center of psychoanalysis. If a patient had an irrational fear of dogs, for example, it was likely because dogs symbolized something traumatic in that person's background.

Of course religions are rife with symbols, and we know that Freud interpreted them as the product of psychosexual development. So, for example, when interpreting Leonardo da Vinci's "Virgin and Child with St. Anne," a painting that depicts the two women doting over the Christ-toddler, Freud focused on the fact that Leonardo himself was an illegitimate child. He therefore had two mothers from whom he wanted attention (his birth-mother and his father's wife), and this wish is symbolized in the painting. In a broader sense, the painting reflects both an infantile desire for maternal affection and an anxiety about who one's real mother is. By consorting with the father, the mother supposedly proves her infidelity to the child! So this is a quintessential example of Freudian analysis. According to Freud, religious symbols acquire power and sustain themselves because they plug into general patterns of individual development and neurosis.

Jung agreed that such symbols are the product of the unconscious, but instead of presenting them as garbled symptoms of pathology, he suggested that they transmitted a universal wisdom that most often eluded the conscious mind. The unconscious, in fact, is the "source of all life," not only because it harbors the drives Freud highlighted (for food, sex, pleasure, mastery, etc.), but also because it contains "the creative seeds of the future and the roots of all constructive fantasies."[18] In encountering the contents of their own psyche, human beings are overwhelmed by its mystery and magnitude; they attribute its products to a divine source and then project them into the world. So, for example, in ancient religions the sun becomes a god because it is emblematic of basic human experiences such as life and death (sunrise and sunset), or our capacities, such as wisdom and discernment (enlightenment, "shedding light on things," etc.). To this extent, Jung agreed with the projection theory of Feuerbach, but unlike Marx and Freud, he thought that these kinds of projections could be transformed into something positive: they provide the gateway to primordial knowledge stored in the unconscious.

When it comes to the symbols we find in dreams, visions, art, and myths, Jung urged us to pay careful attention, because they express the universal patterns of the human psyche. Jung called these patterns *archetypes*, "forms or images of a collective nature which occur practically all over the earth as constituents of myths and at the same time as . . . individual products of unconscious origin."[19] Archetypes are the basic building blocks of meaning, and they take conscious form in "mental images," such as shapes (e.g., circles or triangles), or significant numbers (pairs, threes, fours, or tens). But archetypal images are often more personal or human in nature, such as the mother or father figure, the old sage or the eternal child, the masculine and the feminine, the hero or the savior, or the trickster. In each case, the archetypal image points to a "metaphysical" reality, a truth that "transcends consciousness" and remains "unknowable as such," and this is, for Jung, is the basis of religion.[20]

At the same time, these archetypes represent the accumulated wisdom of humankind, tried and true ways of bestowing meaning and order on human existence. As elements within a body of common, accumulated wisdom, Jung claims that archetypes come from a *collective unconscious*. Even though the symbols representing archetypes may be different depending on the cultural or historical setting, the "analogy" and "sometimes even identity" between them can only arise from a common structure that all human beings share.[21] According to Jung's best guess, archetypes have become part of the permanent structure of our mind, having been passed down from generation to generation, almost like genetic material.

So in the example discussed above, da Vinci's painting, Freud finds only the traces of Leonardo's psychosexual biography. In contrast, Jung uncovers an expression of a universal archetype: the motif of the dual mother or dual descent, which leads to notion of being "twice-born." It is common to find figures in mythology who have both human and divine origins, or who undergo a transition that entails being "adopted" by a second mother. Jung cites the baptism of Jesus as an example, and his disciples followed this precedent and draw upon the same archetypal pattern.[22] Thus da Vinci had delved into the collective unconscious and expressed a fundamental human desire for transformation and rebirth.

This is not to say that Jung's theory focuses entirely on the "collective." In fact, like Otto and James before him, Jung recommended that we emphasize "the original religious experience"[23] of the individual, as opposed to the texts, doctrines, practices, and institutions to which it has given rise. The capacity of individuals to gain access to primordial wisdom, however, has changed radically with the advent of the modern era, which presented a fundamental challenge. The mythic, religious person of yesteryear could say that "something thinks in him" because "[t]he spontaneity of the act of thinking does not lie, causally, in his conscious mind, but in his unconscious."[24] Since the archetypes "thought in him," the "primitive" was in touch with the profound workings of the universal human drama. Collective symbols, myth, and ritual provided the "mental therapy for the sufferings of mankind, such as hunger, war, disease, old age, and death."[25]

In contrast, the modern individual seeks a different form of therapy: rational detachment from both the unconscious and the collective. Mythic thinking still persists in vestigial form (Jung wrote an interesting treatise on UFOs, which he calls a "modern myth," to prove his point), but by distancing themselves from the archetypal unconscious, modern people have cut themselves off from the collective source of life and creativity, "the lower stories of the skyscraper of rational consciousness." So the job of the Jungian therapist is to make that connection once again; otherwise we nervously suspend the psyche in mid-air.[26] What else is therapy, Jung reasoned, than the creation of an individuating, personal myth, one in which the patient could get in touch with powerful symbols and become a hero or heroine—a savior to oneself? And what else is "linking back" to these archetypes but the essence of *re-ligio*?[27]

We should note that Jung's ideas, while themselves well known, have become even more famous in the hands of Joseph Campbell (1904–87). In books such as *The Hero with a Thousand Faces*, *The Masks of God*, and *The Power of Myth*, Campbell reiterated many of Jung's ideas for a popular audience, with an emphasis on the universal commonality of basic motifs in religious traditions the world over. Scholars have questioned this kind of analysis for its tendency to override differences in favor of similarities. Just because both Jesus and the Buddha were hero/saviors, for example, does that mean the meaning of these two figures is the same for their followers? Just because many great religious pilgrimages share similar elements, does that mean they are all the same basic journey?

But an even bigger question presents itself. While figures such as Freud and Marx can be accused of reductionism, that is, transforming religion into something that is in actuality economic or psychosexual in nature, Jung can be found guilty of doing the exact opposite: his theory posits some universal something, some inaccessible quality, feeling, or source, which is the religion's true essence. While one approach might be too simple, the other sounds a lot like a theological defense: the truth behind religion is a uniquely religious thing that is beyond the human capacity to know or analyze it. If the agenda behind the Jungian theory is to rescue and defend myth and religion, then doesn't it violate the phenomenological principles with which he began?

## JUNG

"Religion appears to me to be a peculiar attitude of the human mind, which could be formulated in accordance with the original use of the term 'religio,' that is, a careful consideration and observation of certain dynamic factors, understood to be 'powers,' spirits, demons, gods, laws, ideas, ideals or whatever name man has given to such factors as he has found in his world powerful, dangerous or helpful enough to be taken into careful consideration, or grand, beautiful and meaningful enough to be devoutly adored and loved."[28]

## WHAT TO LOOK FOR:

- The role of preconscious, nonrational dreams, myths, and visions in religious life.

- Universal motifs or archetypes expressed by symbols in different religious traditions: shapes, numbers, or figures of the masculine and the feminine, the child, the old person, the hero/savior, and so on.

- The therapeutic function of religion, especially by means of its myths and symbols.

- The persistence of symbols, myths, and archetypes in modern life (i.e., in dreams, politics, popular culture, etc.).

## Mircea Eliade

Mircea Eliade (1907–1986), a Romanian-born scholar who spent much of his career teaching at the University of Chicago, was one of the true founders of the modern study of religion. While his theories have become controversial in recent years, in part because some scholars see in them a veiled theology, they are still important touchstones in the field.

In one of his most representative works, *The Sacred and the Profane: The Nature of Religion* (1959), Eliade asserts that the essence of religious life is an encounter with the sacred, and he aims to open up the "sacred in its entirety," in all the ways it appears.[29] Eliade begins with some basic assumptions. In keeping with Durkheim, the first thing to say about the sacred is that it is not the profane; it is that which is set aside or different from our everyday, mundane experience. Second, the sacred doesn't just sit there; we experience it because it "shows itself to us." Eliade calls this "act of the manifestation of the sacred" a *hierophany*, literally an "appearance of the sacred/holy."[30] Perhaps the most famous example of a hierophany in the Western tradition is the appearance of the burning bush to Moses. In this story the sacred breaks into the world through a natural object, which is a common occurrence in archaic religion. According to Eliade, an episode like this one is significant because it shows that there is a power and reality that stands outside of ordinary life. Profane existence is characterized by sameness and routine, but the devotee is sensitive to the sacred because it is "really real," as opposed to the banality of the everyday. In fact, "Religious man [*homo religiosus*] thirsts for being," Eliade argues, and only the sacred can quench that thirst.[31]

In Eliade's work, the human response to the sacred generally takes three forms that are themselves intimately tied together: symbol, myth, and ritual.

*Symbol*: As the previous discussion of Freud and Jung indicated, a symbol is something that stands in for something else. A tree in the backyard of your childhood home, for example, might symbolize being innocent and carefree, evoking good memories. But religious symbols are distinctive, according to Eliade, because they make the world of the sacred appear, and they do so in a universal sense. So each individual tree refers to a great mythical tree that holds the whole cosmos together, including the underworld in its roots and the heavens in its branches. Each tree has a sacred quality, because each refers to the sense of order and harmony provided by the original.

*Myth*: Like Jung, Eliade thought that myth was the most fundamental stratum of religious life. The key point about myths is that they convey "a primordial event that took place at the beginning of time."[32] All myths could, in a sense, begin with "Once upon a time . . . " because they relate events that occurred in some ancient, sacred past, at or close to the beginning of the world. They often have to do with creation, sometimes with creation of the universe or human beings, other times with the origins of objects or things we find valuable, powerful, or intriguing. They also provide the paradigm for human behavior. *Homo religiosus*, according to Eliade, is immersed in these models and does little in life without mythic precedent; everything must be done in accordance with what the primordial gods and heroes did in the beginning.

*Ritual*: If myths provide the stories that recapture the sacred origin, then ritual is the conscious, repeated act of following its precedents. So all the features of the ritual take on a symbolic significance. For example, a god or hero might have killed a "marine monster" and "dismembered its body in order to create the cosmos." Now, to consecrate a new beginning of some sort (building a house/temple, starting a journey, beginning a new stage of life, and so on), the religious person might make a sacrifice, symbolically killing the monster, to recapture and "actualize" the sacred beginning once again.[33]

By means of these three functions, the sacred and its appearances come to provide a basic organizing principle for religious adherents.

This becomes all the more clear for Eliade when we examine the manifestation of the sacred in both space and time. For example, "[S]pace," Eliade argues, "is not homogeneous"—it has "breaks in it; some parts of space are qualitatively different from others."[34] This point is easy to grasp. Certain places have an aura around them that marks them off from the everyday, places like the Grand Canyon or the 9/11 memorial site in Lower Manhattan. Sacred spaces also have an aura, but for a specific reason, according to Eliade: they recall the founding of a new world and thus provide a "central axis for all future orientation."[35] Instead of wandering aimlessly, the religious person always has an orienting point around which his or her spatial life is organized.

This center is often thought to be a great mythic pole, pillar, mountain, tree, or some other vertical upright. It can also be a building that marks the spot where an original hierophany took place. Such structures symbolize an axis of the world (an *axis mundi*), which expands outwards in symbolic influence. The original center—the center of the world—radiates its sacrality to outposts (e.g., temples or churches) that are at the center of their own local realms. And this analogy can be taken further. In traditional settings, the home itself is an organizing center, and it takes on a special symbolic value, distinguishing it from the world outside. The last step in this "system of micro-macrocosmic correspondences"[36] might be a room, or even the body. Have you ever thought about how your room is, in a sense, your sacred space? And perhaps you have heard the saying, "the body is a temple"? In each of these cases, from the macro- to the micro-, rituals radiate from the sacred center.

Eliade adds the mythic and ritual dimension to his account of sacred space by recalling actions that must be performed before crossing the threshold of a space, and those that accompany the building of a house or a new temple. Mythic stories accompany these ritual gestures. So if building a house or a local temple is like creating a new world by imposing order on chaos and making a symbolic connection with *the* sacred center, then it should recall an ancient story about the way the world as a whole was founded. This is the way that meaningful, sacred space is created, established, and organized—by recalling some moment when everything got started.

Time is the other basic mode through which the sacred makes itself known. Eliade asserts that "like space," time "is neither homogeneous nor continuous."[37] That is, some days or periods are marked off as special, such as New Year's Day, or even Spring Break. But, again, Eliade claims that sacred time in a religious sense has a distinct quality. In contrast with the ceaseless progress of moments and days and months and years in everyday, profane time, sacred time always refers back to "that time" (*illud tempus*) when the world was founded and the gods performed their legendary deeds. To this extent, when *homo religiosus* enters sacred time, it is like becoming timeless. Especially for "archaic man [or woman]," sacred time is cyclical and "reversible" because it circles back to an "eternal mythical present"[38] that can always be brought back through symbol, myth, and ritual.

Times are first and foremost symbolic, so a day that is just like any other for someone else might be significant for you, like a birthday. When it comes to religious holidays and festivals, the symbolism goes deeper, so the New Year, to take another example, always refers to the creation or recreation of the world, thus rendering it sacred. The symbolic power of a holy time is therefore related to myth. A story of creation gives the content to the sense of renewal and new beginnings, and often these myths are recalled during New Year's celebrations. As we have already discovered, evoking the experience of the sacred is the job of ritual. Often religious traditions will invite some measure of ritual chaos on the night before New Year's, allowing an opportunity for some kind of catharsis or letting go of the old. Then, when the new day dawns, order is re-imposed by invoking the mythic precedents for creation and renewal—and the community can start all over again with a clean slate.

As later critics had pointed out, Eliade's theories led him in controversial directions. For example, he isolated Judaism and Christianity because they maintain a sense of linear, irreversible time, as opposed to the cyclical concept present in many other traditions. In addition, Eliade conceived the sacred and the profane as "two modes of being in the world, two existential situations assumed by man in the course of his history."[39] For *homo religiosus*, "the religious person," the sacred was always there, always within reach. But modern, profane individuals have no such focal point: their time is linear and monotonous; their space is homogeneous, bland, and neutral. While vestiges of the sacred remain, moderns are generally lost because they no longer have a deeper sense of meaning.

As Walter Capps argued, Eliade's phenomenology ultimately led to the conclusion that modern people should in fact attempt to rediscover the sacred and open up this arena once again; to this extent, his theory was intended to have "an important religious function."[40] This means that like Jung, Eliade had an agenda in putting forth his phenomenology of religion, one that perhaps relied on a prior commitment to the reality and necessity of the sacred. Bryan Rennie has written, "*Of course* Eliade was trying to make his readers see, to induce in them the experience of the world of religious structures *as he conceived of it*."[41] Does this mean, in the end, that he also failed to follow phenomenological rules, that his approach was, from the very beginning, far from objective? Or did Eliade's commitment to this method instead *secure* his conclusion about the pervasive human need for the sacred, rendering his theory plausible? This issue is open to considerable debate, but regardless of where you come down on the question, there is no doubt that Eliade's influence is still pervasive in the academic study of religion.

## ELIADE

"Whatever the historical context in which he is placed, *homo religiosus* always believes that there is an absolute reality, the sacred, which transcends this world but manifests itself in this world, thereby sanctifying it and making it real. He further believes that life has a sacred origin and that human existence realizes all of its potentialities in proportion as it is religious—that is, participates in reality. The gods created man and the world, the culture heroes completed the Creation, and the history of all these divine and semidivine works is preserved in myths. By reactualizing sacred history, by imitating the divine behavior, man puts and keeps himself close to the gods—that is, in the real and the significant."[42]

**WHAT TO LOOK FOR:**

- Manifestations of the sacred (hierophanies) in space and time. Space: the feeling of sacred space, rituals surrounding it, the axis mundi ("center of the world"). Time: reversible, repeatable time; *illud tempus, in illo tempore* ("that time," "in that time," i.e., time at the beginning of the world); the "eternal present" of sacred time.

- Mapping the sacred in terms of symbol, myth, and ritual. Symbols reveal a "more real" world behind this one. Myths refer to *illud tempus* ("that time") and set precedents for religious people. Rituals reactualize myths and allow repeated experience of the sacred.

- Universal patterns and motifs of religious life (e.g., trees, stones, fruit, mountains, water, the sun, the moon, buildings, animals, etc.).

- Vestiges of the sacred in contemporary life and human psychology.

## Ninian Smart

Another version of the phenomenological approach comes to us from Ninian Smart (1927–2001), a Scottish-born philosopher of religion who spent much of his career teaching at the University of Lancaster (where, in 1967, he set out to found the first nontheological department of religious studies in England) and the University of California, Santa Barbara. Smart's body of work spanned the full, global range of philosophical, religious, and secular worldviews.

Smart's basic aim is studying religion was to discover "the various ways in which human beings conceive of themselves, and act in the world."[43] To achieve this goal, Smart tells us that we must follow the phenomenological method and start with bracketing, but he is famous for taking a further step. Studying religion also requires a special form of imagination, the *empathetic imagination*, which "tries to bring out what religious acts mean to the actors."[44] Smart uses a vivid image to characterize this connection, which you might recall from Chapter 1: in studying religion, we attempt to find out what it's like to walk a mile in another person's moccasins.[45]

As we noted earlier, this metaphor can be misleading: it does not suggest that the study of religion is about actually *having* the experiences of others. In fact, scholarly empathy must be balanced with distance, and it leads up to a thorough conceptual analysis of any given religious worldview. Like Eliade, Smart attempted to discern patterns in religious life by absorbing the data and then comparing it across the boundaries of cultures and traditions. But in contrast to Eliade, Smart resisted the positing of a single definition or essence (i.e., the transcending reality of the sacred) beneath these patterns. Instead, he avoided monothetic definition and let the patterns—the *dimensions*—of religious worldviews speak for themselves. Taken together, Smart claimed, they "give a kind of functional delineation of religions in lieu of a strict definition."[46]

So what are these dimensions? Smart identified seven features that taken together, assist us in identifying and analyzing religion:

*The ritual or practical dimension.* Religion "involves such activities as worship, meditation, pilgrimage, sacrifice, sacramental rites and healing activities."[47] Worship, contemplation, transformation, and social performance are all important aspects of the ritual dimension. Specific examples include prayer, singing, dancing, chanting, recitation, meditation, pilgrimage, bathing/washing, and so on.

*The doctrinal or philosophical dimension.* Religious traditions often emphasize standard sets of belief and forms of analysis meant to interpret, apply, and elaborate on them. So in exploring this dimension, we look for a creed or declaration of faith; a developed collection of accepted beliefs, transmitted in texts and oral tradition; and groups devoted to the contemplation of core beliefs (e.g., schools of theological thought).

*The mythic or narrative dimension.* "Every religion has its stories."[48] Narrative is almost synonymous with memory for Smart, and it confers a sense of identity for both individuals and groups. Mythic narratives also provide the basis for both ritual and sacred space, articulate both origins and the end of the cosmos, and offer demonstrations of core beliefs. So within religious traditions, we often discover stories of creation, the gods, heroes, the founder, exemplary followers, the afterlife, and/or the end of the world.

*The experiential and emotional dimension.* "[W]e are creatures of flesh and blood, and death, sex, fear, love, pleasure, and so forth" are crucial elements in the religious life,[49] but religious experience also has a calmer, contemplative side. So here we are led to investigate experiences like those described by Otto and James; expressions of emotion in personal and communal settings; mystical experiences of both peace and ecstasy; and the physiological effects of holding certain beliefs and engaging in particular forms of practice.

*The ethical or legal dimension.* What is the right thing to do? All religious traditions seemingly have something to say about this question; they provide authoritative rules and guidelines for living properly, while also spelling out the consequences of one's actions (i.e., reward and punishment) and articulating the attitudes and motivations that should be behind them. In examining this dimension, we look for lists of moral or legal precepts contained in scripture, or those produced by commentators and exemplars; handbooks or guides that set forth rules governing personal or social behavior; and bodies of legal commentary that are consulted and applied.

*The organizational or social dimension.* Developed religions generally have institutions that are designed, in a whole variety of ways, to sustaining the tradition. And these institutions are, in turn, populated by leaders, representatives, officials, functionaries, and laborers who make them work. These are worldly structures that intersect with and overlap with broader political and social realms (e.g., governments). Examples include churches, temples, schools, ashrams, monasteries, meeting houses, compounds, and charitable organizations; along with pastors, priests, gurus, rabbis, imams, shamans, teachers, theologians, and legal scholars.

*The material or artistic dimension.* Finally, religious traditions manifest themselves in the realms of material culture and artistic production. These objects range from the grand to the small, from the elaborate to the simple, from "high art" to kitschy or mass produced items. As Smart himself notes, "A religion or worldview will express itself typically in material creations, from chapels to cathedrals to temples to mosques, from icons and divine statuary to books and pulpits."[50] We could easily add to his list.

As you can see, Smart's dimensions provide an extensive framework for describing religious worldviews. For one thing, they aid in making comparisons across the boundaries of different traditions. How does one tradition compare with another when it comes to each of these dimensions? We should also think about the work these categories do in describing what's going on *within* a tradition or community. "Christianity," for example, is not just one thing, so it can be useful to engage in dimensional comparison of different branches and communities within it. How might a Lutheran community in Minnesota compare to a Southern Baptist congregation when it comes to the experiential or emotional component of the Christian worldview? How do the Eastern Orthodox, Catholic, and Protestant branches differ on the matter of doctrine and belief? And so on.

Smart also emphasizes the dynamic interplay of these dimensions.[51] In reading the summary presented above, you hopefully made some connections: In keeping with Eliade's theory, doesn't a ritual often depend on mythic precedents? And doesn't the ritual evoke some deep emotional and experiential responses? And isn't it related to the central beliefs and doctrines of a worldview? And what about all of the trappings of a ritual, all the material and aesthetic objects? Who leads the ritual, and what kind of social connections are forged? And does any given ritual reinforce certain ideas about right and wrong? Because we can examine the way the different dimensions interact with each other, Smart argues that his theory is more than just a typology; it also gives us a method for charting change and development within a religious worldview. To put it succinctly, change through time in a tradition is the product of the shifting relationships between these elements.

As useful as it is, not all observers are convinced by Smart's version of phenomenology. The call for empathetic imagination, for example, still seems to hand over considerable authority to the insider, calling to mind the dilemmas associated with the insider–outsider problem, discussed in Chapter 2. Do we really have to see the world the way the insider sees it to understand his or her religious tradition? And who will decide whether we have really walked in his or her moccasins or not, or if we have done it for long enough? In addition, the dimensions themselves seem rather general, and perhaps they already imply a prior definition of religion. For example, can we think of any religious tradition that does not have a *social* dimension? And what exactly distinguishes a religious manifestation of the social, from a nonreligious one?

These are potent challenges, but Smart was firm in his conviction that the scholar, employing the dimensional analysis, has an authoritative take on religion—and one that is in many ways *better* than that of insider. This is not because the phenomenologist has seen some sort of singular mystical essence; instead, the observer following in Smart's footsteps (moccasins?) simply has some very good tools for generating helpful working definitions, thick descriptions, effective explanations, and productive comparisons. And thus religions emerge as unique combinations of a variety of possible factors; they are complex worldviews tied together by sets of distinct characteristics, but through dimensional analysis, we can see where their resemblances overlap.

## SMART

"The history of religions . . . involves depicting histories, but in a manner which involves empathy . . . [It] is delicate and has a sensitive soul . . . a distancing, and yet a warmth; objectivity and yet subjectivity of spirit; description but also evocation; method, but also imagination."[52]

"From history and from comparative study of religions we can begin to piece together the so-to-say logical structure of systems—how the differing dimensions of religion . . . are bound to one another in relations of implication and suggestion, of expression and definition; also, too, how within the range of doctrines in a system they are mutually related and organically influence one another."[53]

## WHAT TO LOOK FOR:

- Religion as a worldview alongside others, e.g., philosophical or secular/political visions.

- The results of employing the empathetic imagination: what would it be like to walk a mile in another person's shoes?

- Comparison between and within religious worldviews drawing on seven dimensions: ritual/practical, doctrinal/philosophical, mythic/narrative, experiential/emotional, ethical/legal, institutional/social, and material/artistic.

## Back to Theology?

As you have discovered, the academic study of religion owes a great deal to the Enlightenment effort to prioritize rational, scholarly analysis over nonrational belief or feeling. This legacy has led to a distinction between the perspective of the religious insider and the viewpoint of the religious studies scholar. The discussion in Chapter 2 captured this divide by describing several Orders of Meaning in the study of religion. The First Order, the immediate, is constituted by what insiders do, say, and feel while they are in the thick of things religiously; the Second Order, the reflective, is the level of insider reflection on the immediate, and theology is one of its components; and the Third Order is that of the academic outsider: the theories we have been investigating by and large take a place at this level. But sometimes the boundaries get blurred. In particular, we have noted instances where theology (which resides within the Second Order of Meaning) seems to creep into the theories that have been so formative in constituting the field—probably because the contemporary study of religion owes as much to Christian theology as it does to the Enlightenment.

Now we have to add yet another wrinkle. Some forms of Christian theology have adjusted to accommodate both post-Enlightenment ideas and the plurality of world religions. Many "orthodox" or "fundamentalist" theologians have wanted little to do with the academic study of religion,[54] but others have felt the impact of both modern, nonreligious thought and the diversity and richness of non-Christian forms. In response, they have generated theories that were born of theology but have wider currency in the field as a whole. There's no better example of this development than Paul Tillich, who perhaps still "remains the unacknowledged theoretician of our entire enterprise [the academic study of religion]."[55]

## Paul Tillich

Tillich (1886–1965) was a German theologian who left his homeland before the Second World War and came to the United States. He held teaching posts at Union Theological Seminary in New York, Harvard Divinity School, and the University of Chicago, but he also reached large audiences through his popular books and public lectures. His theoretical perspective, which responded to the challenge of existentialism, was decisively Christian, but it is also applicable to other traditions because religion in general, Tillich suggested, is a matter of being grasped by an *ultimate concern*.

First we need to consider *existentialism*. You will recall that the concept of alienation was decisive for figures such as Hegel, Feuerbach, and Marx. Twentieth-century European existentialists built on this idea. The first thing we can say about ourselves, they proposed, is that we *are*, that we exist in the world. Next we have to acknowledge that we are finite and mortal, that we are going to die. In the face of these circumstances, we are faced with an urgent decision. How are we going to be? What projects are we going to set for ourselves, knowing that our time is limited? This situation causes anxiety because our decision can seem so arbitrary. It is often out of our control, the product of external forces and other people's decisions, and then we think, "Why this option and not the others?" Every action we undertake excludes an infinite number of other possibilities. Perhaps we manage to stand up to this horrible freedom and make a resolute choice . . . but in the end, we still die. So isn't it all meaningless?

These questions are not cheery, and many existentialist thinkers gave us no exit. Most of the ways people try to respond to these challenges, they claimed, are purely escapist. The masses get wrapped up in their lives, distract themselves with entertainment, chatter, and everyday routine; and they devise their various life projects and myths about themselves. All the while they remain denial about the real circumstances of our existence. Religion, they claimed, was a prime culprit in promoting this blindness: it frees us from responsibility of genuine decision-making by telling us what we are and what we should do. Then it proposes that there is some way to overcome or transcend death itself. According to the existentialist, this is all illusory and inauthentic. The only way to deal with the tragic nature of life is to confront it head-on.

Figures such as Tillich opened themselves up to this challenge but had a very different response. Tillich agreed that existentialism had posed some powerful questions, but he claimed that religion, and Christianity in particular, does in fact provide an answer. Tillich affirmed that humankind suffers from a "tragic estrangement from [its] true being" that causes a spiritual "emergency."[56] He also agreed with the secular, philosophical existentialists that a lot of what generally counts as religion—indeed, a lot of what most people consider fulfilling in general—does not actually speak to our existential situation. For the most part we are occupied with what Tillich calls "preliminary concerns," which include the trivial aspects of everyday existence, the individual concerns that seem important (such as exams, degrees, jobs, money, romance, etc.), and even the grander preoccupations of humankind (art, science, or politics).[57] Even religious people often get hung up on preliminaries. They suppose that everything hinges on the intellect, action, or emotion,[58] or maybe they get absorbed by the politics of their church, temple, or synagogue. Perhaps they go through the motions during rituals, recite scripture by rote memory without reflecting on its meaning, or get fixated on a holy object while forgetting what's behind it. Fleeing into the world of preliminary concerns is a constant enticement, given the human condition.

In contrast, however, the essence of religion is an "ultimate concern." It is "independent of any conditions of character, desire, or circumstance"; it is "total," inescapable, and "infinite"; and "no moment or relaxation and rest is possible in the face of a religious concern which is ultimate, unconditional, total, and infinite."[59] The core of religious life is an absolute commitment, but it is not an escape, as the secular existentialist would suggest. In fact, in the face of a world that constantly threatens us with death and meaninglessness, taking on an ultimate concern is the ultimate risk. It takes courage to concern oneself not solely with the preliminary things of this world, but primarily with something unconditional, total, and absolute. In other words, taking on an ultimate concern is a leap of faith— but it's an existential leap, the only truly authentic decision one can make about how one is going to be in the world.

Of course, Tillich argues, this concern is about *something*. In his theology this something is called "the ground of Being," *"that which determines our being or not-being."*[60] This unconditioned content eludes human concepts or representation but is generally associated with "God." Tillich also tells us that his main purpose as a Christian theologian is to affirm the "New Being," Jesus Christ. Nevertheless, if we expand Tillich's ideas, as he himself did later in his life, the name we use for the object of religious concern is in some sense arbitrary, and its content may vary, as long as it is in fact ultimate ("unconditional, total, and infinite") for those who are grasped by it. To this extent, it is possible to identify ultimate concern in any religious worldview worth its salt—and this is the way Tillich's theological concept transmutes into a theory and definition of religion in general.

To illustrate this transformation from theology to theory, you might think about "ultimate concern" as follows: ask yourself, why are you reading this book?[61] One possibility is that you are doing so simply because you have to, because it was assigned for a class. In that case, your concern is preliminary because it is related to a limited (but important) goal within the educational system. Perhaps your answer is "I am curious about the study of religion, what it does and where it came from." That's a good response, but it is still preliminary: it has to do with your intellectual curiosity about a bounded area of human knowledge. Now, if you respond, "I am trying to understand how to go about learning the secret of living fully," then you are raising "a religious or ultimate question," because "[a] religious answer relates to the most profound meaning of one's existence."[62]

This is not to say that Tillich excluded the vast world of preliminaries from his analysis. In fact, he based much of his theology on a "method of correlation," which identifies the instances where the preliminary concern becomes "a medium, a vehicle, pointing beyond itself," that is, toward the ultimate concern.[63] As you might imagine, this means that symbols are once again a focus, as they were for Freud, Jung, Eliade, and others. Tillich reminds us that the most basic function of symbols is to "point beyond themselves to something else," but they are distinct from every-day signs (like a stop light) because (1) they participate in the reality they represent (e.g., a president represents his nation but is also part of it), and (2) they reveal "levels of reality which otherwise are closed for us."[64] So there's no way to know what it means for something to be profoundly beautiful, for example, without the symbols (in poetry, music, or paintings, for example) that take us there. Of course, words always point to some-thing besides themselves, and ultimate concern always finds a name for itself—"God," for example, and all the characteristics commonly attrib-uted to divine beings (power, love, justice, etc.). But symbols also take more concrete form. Tillich was fascinated by the way both myth and the arts can point to and participate in "the depth dimension of reality itself, the dimension of reality which is the ground of every other dimension and every other depth . . . the ultimate power of being."[65]

For Tillich (and for figures such as Jung and Eliade as well) existential-ism had accurately characterized the plight of modern people. We find ourselves alienated from our own experience, wandering in a meaning-less world, hungry for the "really real" truth of our existence that has been lost. Jung and Eliade presented generalized notions of that "really real" that had a theological ring to them. But Tillich's answer to the existential-ist challenge that faced all modern people was distinctively Christian. This leads us to difficult issues that come with playing on the border of the Second Order of Meaning (theology) and the Third Order of Meaning (the academic study of religion). Does Tillich's Christian commitment disqualify his theories? Or did he reach out far enough from his position on the inside to render his theory and valid and useful for the nonconfessional student or nonreligious scholar? Once again, these are important matters, and they need to be considered. At the very least, Tillich offers you an intrigu-ing theoretical idea that is definitely worth experimenting with: ultimate concern. What *is* the ultimate concern that grasps any given individual, community, or tradition that you might encounter? Discovering an answer to this question—while not always easy—can provide an excellent starting point for understanding and further inquiry.

## TILLICH

"The concept of religion which makes . . . a large extension of the meaning of the term possible is the following. Religion is the state of being grasped by an ultimate concern, a concern which qualifies all other concerns as preliminary and which itself contains the answer to the question of the meaning of our life . . . The predominant religious name for the content of such concern is God—a god or gods. In nontheistic religions divine qualities are ascribed to a sacred object or an all-pervading power or a highest principle such as the Brahma or the One. In secular quasi-religions the ultimate concern is directed towards objects like nation, science, a particular form or stage of society, or a highest ideal of humanity, which are then considered divine."[66]

## WHAT TO LOOK FOR:

- The ultimate concern within a given religious tradition taken as a whole, or according to the report and understanding of the individual practitioner.

- The way in which ultimate concern is symbolized in words, myths, and art.

- The expression and acting out of ultimate concern in seemingly nonreligious ways.

- A tradition or community's response to existential dilemmas: why are we here, and how should we confront death?

## Wilfred Cantwell Smith

The final figure treated in this chapter brings us back to one of the classic principles in the study of religion, articulated all the way back in Chapter 1: "He who knows one knows none." In his most famous work,

*The Meaning and End of Religion*, theologian Wilfred Cantwell Smith (1916–2000) agreed and wrote, "One has not understood religion if one's interpretation is applicable to only one of its forms." But then he added, "neither has one understood religion if one's interpretation does justice only to some abstraction of religiousness in general but not to the fact that for most men [and women] of faith, loyalty and concern are not for any such abstraction but quite specifically and perhaps even exclusively for their own unique tradition—or even for one section within that."[67] With his emphasis on individual faith over intellectual abstractions, Smith's work raises important questions—not the least of which is whether an "academic" examination of religion is desirable in the first place.

In *The Meaning and End of Religion*, Smith engages in persistent criticism of abstraction and generalization. As we saw in Chapter 2, he objects to the general term "religion" itself, for example, because it allows us to disengage from "out-reaching faith."[68] In addition, Smith notes that a general concept of "religion" or "religions" is particular to the Euro-American context. While other traditions name themselves, they do so in their own terms; they generally do not attempt to extend their own vocabulary to other traditions. In keeping with its tendency to transform religion into a "thing," Western scholarship has generally failed to use native terms for other traditions and has instead made up its own labels, such as Buddhism, Hinduism, Judaism, Taoism, Confucianism, and so on.

As Smith notes, "Hinduism" is a particularly interesting and problematic example. The British invented this concept as a catch-all to contend with an incredibly diverse range of doctrines and practices they found in India during the era of colonialism. The term "Hinduism," Smith argues, implies that all of these diverse forms are somehow part of the same "system," but in actuality, "the mass of religious phenomena that we shelter under the umbrella of that term . . . Is not a unity and does not aspire to be."[69] So in this case, the outsider category imposes a unity where it does not actually exist.

When it comes to China, however, outsider categories clearly divide. In the Chinese context, an individual may engage in some practices that could be called "Confucian," others that would be considered "Taoist," and still others that are "Buddhist"—all within the space of a day, an hour, or even less. Given this way of dividing up the world, it is difficult to "imagine how a person can 'belong to three different religions' . . . at the same time." But here is the key point: "The perplexity arises not from something confused and bizarre about China so much as from the conceptualization of religious systems."[70] It's the categorization—the suggestion that "Confucianism," "Buddhism," and "Taoism" are three absolutely distinct things—that causes the problems, not what's happening on the ground.

Smith provides a provocative basis for criticizing the terms and concepts we use in sorting out religious phenomena. But what is his positive program? What theory, or counter-theory of religion does he offer? As we have seen, Smith was concerned that abstractions distract us from the real heart of religion. He likened quasi-scientific observers to "flies crawling on the outside of a goldfish bowl," counting up the scales on the fish but "never finding out, how it feels to be a goldfish."[71] If religion is seen as an abstract system, then the observer becomes fixated on external trappings and a fixed, static notion of a tradition, while overlooking diversity and transformation within it. Even more importantly, according to Smith, we must understand the "system" as an expression of a core experience, which is individual and deeply personal. In short, "[t]o know 'a religion' is not yet to know the religious life of him whom one observes."[72] The student or scholar must instead aim "to discover and make known the personal faith of men that [religious] traditions have served."[73]

Smith's recommendations may not be persuasive for many because he had theological purpose in making them. As we saw in the Chinese example above, objectifying religion tends to produce and solidify differences between traditions, leading to tension and conflict. Smith hoped that a more nuanced comparison would lead to an appreciation of a common bond that is shared by all religions. At the same time, Smith worried that the objectification of religion leads to "malaise," meaning that conceiving it as a general system and as an "ism" compartmentalizes it as just one part of life, when it should be understood as an all-encompassing concern. In other words, conceptualizing religion detracts from faith.

Despite this theological impulse behind Smith's critique, his basic lesson is clear, and in the decades since the publication of *The Meaning and End of Religion*, many scholars have followed up on it. Smith was a forerunner in reminding us that we must be aware of our categories—even if they seem to be obvious and given—because they have the potential to produce distortion, misunderstanding, and indifference.

## W. C. SMITH

"What is profoundly important in the religious life of any people . . . is that, whatever else it may be, religious life is a kind of life. Participants know this, consciously or unconsciously. Observers have to learn it. In learning it, they find that they must leave behind the distraction of congealed concepts postulating entities different from the living persons before them, or even theoretically independent of them . . . The observer's concept of religion is by definition constituted of what can be observed. Yet the whole pith and substance of religious life lies in its relation to what cannot be observed."[74]

## WHAT TO LOOK FOR:

- Heartfelt expressions of individual faith and piety.

- The power of individual spirituality to promote change and development in a religious tradition.

- The power of individual faith to generate the most important expressions of a religious tradition.

- Native terms used to characterize, name, and describe a religious tradition.

- Places where general categories or labels fail to capture the complexity and particularity of religious phenomena.

## Conclusion: Back to Plato's Cave

So where does religion ultimately reside, inside Plato's cave, or out? In this chapter you have read about some strikingly different responses, which we can place on a continuum. At one end we find theorists such as Feuerbach, Marx, and Freud, who interpreted religious beliefs as projections, as illusory shadows on the wall that keep people distracted from what's really true. On the other side we have figures such as Tillich and Smith, who, while different from each other, generally agreed that the essence of religion shines forth and makes life worth living. Somewhere in the middle (but leaning toward Tillich and Smith's side) are figures such as Jung and Eliade. Religions, they claimed, carry within them some essential, unique, universal truth that we need to recapture, but the observer should attempt to maintain a methodological distance to establish a firm foundation for his or her conclusions. (Perhaps only Ninian Smart occupies a true middle ground in this range of theorists.)

Once again, the jury is still out on who is right in this big debate. After all, we are talking here about whether religion in general or any given religion is true or not. It's not clear that such a debate could *ever* be resolved to everyone's satisfaction. Fortunately, however, we do not have to come to a conclusion about this weighty matter to discern the usefulness of the theories surveyed in this chapter. Marx was right: it is very difficult to understand religion, in many of its manifestations, without taking account of economic conditions. And religion *is* interwoven with individual psychology, the body, sexuality, and our desires, as Freud would have it. It is a wellspring of myths and symbols that tells us something deep about what is meaningful for human beings (Jung); it helps many people organize space and time in meaningful ways (Eliade). And finally, as Tillich and W. C. Smith would tell us, it does seem to *grasp* many of its followers in a way that is different from everyday concerns.

In this chapter (and the last), we have been working with these kinds of theoretical ideas, and hopefully it is obvious by now that such ideas have staying power because each has a distinctive value in the understanding and interpretation of religious phenomena. It is now up to you, the beginning student of religion, to apply these theories—to bring them out into the field—so they can be tested, evaluated, modified, fine-tuned—and, if this is what your judgment dictates, rejected. The point of this process is, as we suggested earlier, the process itself. Engaging in it establishes provisional but reliable knowledge about the subject matter and opens the way for further progress, innovation, and discovery.

This point will become clear in the next chapter, in which we will take account of more recent trends in the academic study of religion. These perspectives and areas of investigation not only build upon and draw upon the classic theories that we have been discussing, but they also signal new possibilities as the field moves into its future.

## Notes

1. Karl Marx and Frederick Engels, *The German Ideology: Part One*, ed. C. J. Arthur (New York: International Publishers, 1986), 37.
2. Ibid., 42.

3. Ibid., 123.

4. Karl Marx, "Contribution to the Critique of Hegel's Philosophy of Right: Introduction," in *The Marx-Engels Reader*, 2nd ed., ed. Robert C. Tucker (New York and London: W. W. Norton, 1978), 53–54.

5. Ibid., 54

6. Marx and Engels, *The German Ideology: Part One*, 64.

7. Marx, "Contribution to the Critique of Hegel's Philosophy of Right," 53–54.

8. See Sigmund Freud, *The Future of an Illusion*, trans. James Strachey (New York and London: W. W. Norton, 1961), 44.

9. Ibid., 10, 13.

10. Ibid., 15–16.

11. Jerry S. Piven, "Death, Neurosis, and Normalcy: On the Ubiquity of Person and Social Delusions," *Journal of the American Academy of Religion* 71, no. 1 (March 2003): 148.

12. Freud, *The Future of an Illusion,* 37.

13. Ibid., 24.

14. Ibid., 49.

15. Diane Jonte-Pace, "Introduction: Teaching Freud and Religion," in *Teaching Freud*, ed. Diane Jonte-Pace (Oxford and New York: Oxford University Press, 2003), 4.

16. Freud, *The Future of an Illusion,* 43.

17. C. G. Jung, *Psychology and Religion* (New Haven and London: Yale University Press, 1938), 3.

18. Robert A. Segal (ed.), *Encountering Jung: Jung on Mythology* (Princeton, NJ: Princeton University Press, 1998), 56.

19. Ibid., 63.

20. C. G. Jung, *Answer to Job*, 2nd ed., trans. R. F. C. Hill (Princeton, NJ: Princeton University Press, 1973), xii.

21. Ibid., 63–64.

22. Ibid., 67–69.

23. Jung, *Psychology and Religion*, 7.

24. Segal, *Encountering Jung*, 83.

25. Ibid., 95.

26. Ibid., 41.

27. Ibid., 126.

28. Jung, *Psychology and Religion*, 5.

29. Mircea Eliade, *The Sacred and the Profane: The Nature of Religion*, trans. Willard R. Trask (San Diego and New York: Harcourt Brace Jovanovich, 1959), 10.

30. Ibid., 11.

31. Ibid., 64.

32. Ibid., 95.

33. Ibid., 100.

34. Ibid., 20.

35. Ibid., 21.

36. Ibid., 169.

37. Ibid., 68.

38. Ibid., 70.

39. Ibid., 14.

40. Walter Capps, *Religious Studies: The Making of a Discipline* (Minneapolis, MN: Fortress Press, 1995), 145.

41. Bryan Rennie, "Mircea Eliade: 'Secular Mysticism' and the History of Religions," *Religion* 38 (2008): 336.

42. Eliade, *The Sacred and the Profane*, 202.

43. Ninian Smart, *Religions of Asia* (Englewood Cliffs, NJ: Prentice Hall, 1993), 32.

44. Ninian Smart, *Dimensions of the Sacred: An Anatomy of the World's Beliefs* (Berkeley and Los Angeles: University of California Press, 1996), 2.

45. Smart, *Religions of Asia*, 11, 17.

46. Smart, *Dimensions of the Sacred*, 7.

47. Ibid., 10.

48. Ibid.

49. Ibid., 132–3.

50. Ibid., 11.

51. Ibid., 7.

52. Ninian Smart, *Beyond Ideology: Religion and the Future of Western Civilization* (San Francisco: Harper & Row, 1981), 47.

53. Ninian Smart, *Concept and Empathy: Essay in the Study of Religion*, ed. Donald Wiebe (New York: New York University Press, 1986), 74–75.

54. See Paul Tillich, *Systematic Theology: Volume 1* (Chicago: University of Chicago Press, 1951), 3–4.

55. J. Z. Smith, "Connections," in *On Teaching Religion*, ed. Christopher I. Lehrich (Oxford and New York: Oxford University Press, 2013), 54.

56. Paul Tillich, *Theology of Culture*, ed. Robert C. Kimball (New York: Oxford University Press, 1959), 9.

57. Tillich, *Systematic Theology: Volume 1*, 12.

58. Paul Tillich, *Dynamics of Faith* (New York: Harper & Row, 1957), 30–40.

59. Tillich, *Systematic Theology: Volume 1*, 11–12.

60. Ibid., 14.
61. The following example is adapted from Frederick J. Streng, *Understanding Religious Life*, 3rd ed. (Belmont, CA: Wadsworth, 1984), 7.
62. Ibid.
63. Tillich, *Systematic Theology: Volume 1*, 13.
64. Tillich, *Dynamics of Faith*, 41–43.
65. Tillich, *Theology of Culture*, 59.
66. Paul Tillich, *Christianity and the Encounter of the World Religions* (New York and London: Columbia University Press, 1963), 4–5.
67. Wilfred Cantwell Smith, *The Meaning and End of Religion* (Minneapolis, MN: Fortress Press, 1991), 3.
68. Ibid., 13.
69. Ibid., 66.
70. Ibid., 67–68.
71. Ibid., 7.
72. Ibid., 135.
73. Ibid., 188–89.
74. Ibid., 136.

# 5 Contemporary Trends in the Field

In the last two chapters, we have surveyed a set of influential theories within the academic study of religion. These intellectual frameworks are "classic" in the sense that they have been important in the development of the field, but they appear in this book mostly because we still talk about them: books, articles, conferences, and classes are still abuzz with Otto, James, Durkheim, Weber, Turner, Geertz, Marx, Freud, Jung, Eliade, Smart, Tillich, and the Smiths (W. C. and J. Z.). Scholars continue to apply the theoretical ideas of these figures, with the intention of making discoveries, explaining emerging and previously under-investigated cases, and moving our general understanding of religion(s) forward. Even when these frameworks are subject to criticism, they remain influential because they provide a stepping stone for something new.

This chapter is devoted to contemporary trends that have responded to, built on, and, in many cases, departed from classic theories. There was no way that most of our thinkers in Chapters 3 and 4 could have taken account of the pressures of globalization, the pervasiveness of the media, developments in technology, discoveries in science, and environmental consciousness. And as products of their time and place, most of these theorists were also not sensitive to issues of gender, race, ethnicity, and sexual orientation. So, as the world has changed, and as the demands of scholarship have expanded, the contemporary study of religion has picked up where these theorists left off.

In this chapter we move from the classic to the cutting-edge with a survey of topics that occupy the attention of many contemporary scholars. This summary is necessarily selective and relatively brief, but it does offer a reasonably accurate portrait of the field as it stands, and along the way, it also presents you with some intriguing prospects for further exploration.

## The Study of Religion Itself: Always in Question

As this book has often shown, the nature of the study of religion is still a complicated issue; debates and controversies continue to rage. We have seen that definitions and even the desirability of using the term "religion" are contested matters. The disciplinary orientation of the field is also much discussed. In this book you have encountered theologians, psychologists, philosophers, sociologists, anthropologists, historians— and some who defy categorization. What academic approach should strike the tone? Should we think of this field as scientific, as humanistic (that is, as we might think about the study and appreciation of literature or art), as philosophical, or even as somehow therapeutic—or as some combination? The jury is still out. The study of religion also has its unique connection with theology to wrestle with, as we saw in Chapter 2, and this legacy continues to present an challenge. At the same time, the modern, post-Enlightenment secular tradition in Europe and America is also a basic premise for the religious studies enterprise—and this influence is not without its controversy.

These and other concerns have given rise to ever more rigorous forms of self-reflection. Think back to our theorists in Chapters 3 and 4, for example. You might have noticed that a lot of them were Germans, and all of them were of European or American descent. Almost all of them came from a Christian background (Freud and Marx are important exceptions), and many were Protestant. Does this matter? Many would argue that it does, because the field is still pervaded with biases that can be traced to its originators. Critics have noted, for example, that we continue to emphasize texts, beliefs, and private experiences in our explorations—central aspects within some influential forms of Protestantism—over oral culture, performance, ritual, embodiment, community, and public expression. Old habits die hard, these critics tell us: while making claims to neutrality, objectivity, and openness, the academic study of religion is still constricted by very particular Western, Christian assumptions.

In addition, as Europeans and Americans, all of our theorists were members of cultures that engaged in colonialism, the occupation of the so-called Third World for political and economic gain. Their intellectual approach was therefore built on a basic assumption, namely, that the scholar stands above the material he or she is investigating. One variation on this theme has been called *Orientalism*. According to Edward Said, Orientalism is "a Western style for dominating, restructuring, and having authority over the Orient."[1] For centuries, Said argued, attitudes associated with Orientalism have had a negative effect on the representation of the cultures of Asia, from the Middle East to the Far East, in the interest in propping up the idea of Euro-American superiority. Has the connection between scholarship and colonialism affected the way that the religions of the world—particularly non-Christian traditions—are viewed? It seems inevitable. Some argue, for example, that Europeans and Americans often think about Asian traditions as mystical, dreamy, irrational, passive, and effeminate because this characterization highlights the contrasting identity of the Westerner as clear-headed, rational, active, and masculine—and thus fit to rule over the lands of "the East." Entrenched views such as this one, it is claimed, continue to distort our thinking.[2]

The intellectual imperialism of European and American scholars has also influenced our conceptual organization of movements and traditions. Many of us accept as a given, for example, that there is a line-up of "world religions" (which includes Christianity, Judaism, Hinduism, Buddhism, Islam, Confucianism, and Taoism) and an accompanying array of "minor" ones (such as Yoruba, Sikhism, Jainism, Zoroastrianism, and so on). But where did this terminology and organizational scheme come from? Historical detective work reveals that these categories were not "native": scholars *invented* them over the last two centuries, in the midst of colonialism. How can we avoid the conclusion that the idea of "world religions," and the definition of individual traditions within this framework, is skewed?[3]

Perhaps, as W. C. Smith and others have suggested, the desire to pin down individual religions—and to pin down religion itself—by means of some singular, defining characteristic, is the bigger problem. One implication of *postmodern* theory is the suggestion that this kind of *essentialism* is (a) fictional and (b) linked to some kind of power play (e.g., the politics of colonialism). So, according to this theory, there is no such unity behind what we generally call a "religious tradition," and no single definition of it: it is plural and diverse, especially (following W. C. Smith) if we take account of the lived experience of individuals. At the very least, some would say, let's be sure to talk about "Christianities," "Judaisms," "Hinduisms," "Islams," and so on, in the plural, in order to account for the complexity and richness of the reality that these terms represent.

Indeed, as we have seen in Chapter 2, narrowing down something called "religion" to a single essence often leads to trouble, and according to critics, it is the persistent but misguided error that drives the whole discipline.[4] This claim seems to have some merit. Just recall how often the theorists in previous chapters tried to nail down an absolute essence, that which is *sui generis* ("of its own kind") in religion the world over. While this quest might be compelling, it can also lead to simplification and reductionism. As we have seen, identifying religion as the worship of God/gods is an essentialism that has misleading results, but perhaps the same could be said of boiling it down to "the holy," "the sacred," the "liminal," the "collective unconscious," or "ultimate concern."

These controversies—debates about definition, disciplinary approach, and the persistence of bias—continue unabated. Although it might run the risk of essentialism to say so, these debates are *intrinsic* to the field; they come with the territory. As a result, the contemporary student of religion must incorporate questions such as the following into his or her inquiry: *How much does the European/American legacy of religious studies affect the way it approaches traditions from the rest of the world? Does the academic study of religion still bear the imprint of a particular religious perspective? What is missed by searching for a singular, universal essence of a tradition, or religion and in general? Can we use general labels in the study of religion in a way that avoids their potential pitfalls?*

## Women and Gender

In addition to their relatively homogeneous national and religious identities, you might have noticed something else about the classic theorists surveyed in Chapters 3 and 4: they were all men. We might like to hope that this is irrelevant, but here it does matter, because it tells about who was designated to do academic work up until recent times: men. In addition, the gender identity of those in the field is potentially related to one of its fundamental biases. Women's experience and the conceptualization of gender have not been prominent on the research agenda until the last few decades, and when these issues have been discussed, the analysis has most often been distorted by gender-biased assumptions.

In the wake of feminist movements in the 1970s and 1980s, scholars have worked to remedy this problem by asserting the importance of women's experience, and then by reaching for even broader analysis of religion and gender.[5] In the first stage, in works such as *In Memory of Her* by Elizabeth Schüssler Fiorenza, for example, feminist scholars reminded the world that women played a vital role in the origination and development of major religious traditions—in this case, Fiorenza investigated the prominence of women in the early Christian movement.[6]

In recent years, however, the inquiry has taken another step forward. Lisbaeth Mikaelsson summarizes this advance: "From early on it was realized that a one-sided focus on women will not explain their status and allotted sphere of activity. The category of 'woman' is culturally constructed in relation to the category of 'man'; therefore women will have to be analyzed with a view to the social matrix which produces gender difference."[7] Thus scholars have moved from the most basic, necessary gesture—recovering what had been left out, and thus "changing the subject" to account for women[8]—to a theoretical analysis that makes gender in general an aspect of any thorough treatment of religious phenomena.

In a broad sense, gender is a vital issue in the study of any culture. Feminists have reminded us that there is a distinction between *sex* and *gender*: whereas sex is a physiological distinction, gender is a cultural construction that builds on and extrapolates from sex differences—and religion has been a crucial component in this construction. While women as a sex are half the population, and thus in this basic sense represent half of the adherents of any given religious community, again and again we find that *patriarchy* determines the conception of gender: the roles and identity that are assigned on the basis of sex. Within patriarchal systems, for example, men hold the power, possess the authority, and are thought to have the defining, central experience. Women are perceived as tangential, secondary, and in need of control; their roles are restricted, their voices are silenced, and they are even identified as distracting temptresses or petty instigators. This reconstruction of physiological reality—along with the patriarchal assumptions of those engaged in scholarly investigation—has most often led to the marginalization of women's experience in the academic study of religion, until recent times.

Thinking about the construction of gender in general—the way that being a man or woman is understood, enforced, performed, and imagined—has become an important concern. This construction takes place at the level of personal and social conduct, and within the symbolic or theological imagination. So "gendering" religious studies means that we attend to the different ways that women and men experience and conceive of their identity. It also requires us to analyze their roles (e.g., men are supposed to engage in public life and women are tied to the domestic; different religious duties and practices are assigned to men and women; and so on), with particular sensitivity to the distribution of power and authority—who is allowed and enabled to do what in any given community.

In addition, we must also look at the conceptual or symbolic realm to see the connections—or disconnects—between this realm and everyday experience. For example, while some traditions hold fast to the notion that God or ultimate reality is beyond gender, the imaging of God, gods, and goddesses as male and female is everywhere. The gender of prominent characters in the tradition, from myth and history, is also an important factor in the symbolic imagination, and many traditions uphold basic philosophical schemes that pin down and define the masculine and the feminine (e.g., the yin/yang scheme in Chinese religions). But what difference does this make for men and women in their actual, lived experience? In some communities female goddesses are revered, but women are treated terribly (at least by contemporary, secular standards). On the other hand, devotion to a masculine god does not always entail negative concepts of feminine sex and gender. In some schemes gendered depictions and descriptions might seem to be derogatory (e.g., the feminine as weak, dark, and passive in Taoism), but they turn out to be indications of an alternative source of power that must be acknowledged and channeled.

The interrelationship between the symbolic realm, social roles, and individual experience is complex indeed, but taken together, the modes of analysis that we have discussed—discovering the distinct experiences of men and women; analyzing personal and social roles, authority, power relations; examining the symbolic and theological content—allow us to "engender" the study of religion and reverse its long-standing suppression of this issue. And in the most basic terms, "changing the subject" to take account of gender is one way to ensure that the fullness of the subject matter is before us, and not just part of it. As a result, we need to keep asking: *How might focusing on women alter our theoretical approach? What role do women play in any given community, is their experience distinctive, and how has their tradition contributed to the way gender is understood in the cultures to which they belong? What roles and expectations follow from being a man or a woman, and who is in charge of what sphere of life? And what is the relationship between these arrangements of authority and roles and the symbolic, conceptual content of a tradition?*

## Sexuality, the Body, and Orientation

"Changing the subject" in religious studies to reflect women's experience has been accompanied by careful reflection on sex, sexuality, and the body. For one thing, it is clear that once we start thinking about sex and gender, we must also think about expressions of sexuality and relationships that are thought to be normative, and those that are not. As a consequence, the examination of gender and sexuality is intertwined with attention to gay, lesbian, and transgender people and their perspectives.

As was the case with "changing the subject" to address women's experience, "que(e)rying religion"[9] has first and foremost aimed to recapture gay, lesbian, and transgender experience in religious contexts. This move is closely aligned with challenging the *heteronormativity* of the field—the basic assumption that the traditional heterosexual model of love, relationship, and marriage is standard and normal, while all other arrangements are marginal and deviant. It is obvious that until quite recently, this challenge was hardly thought to be worth considering. Scholars once again seemingly colluded with the traditions that they studied, which by and large prohibited homosexuality and enforced highly constrained identities and roles for men and women. But here too the field has begun to open up, with recognition of those who had previously been silenced, recovery and re-reading of relevant themes in sacred texts and theology, comparative examination of Lesbian, Gay, Bisexual, Transgender, Queer (LGBTQ) experience in different settings, and social scientific analysis of LGBTQ communities.[10] These forms of inquiry once again reveal a whole territory that was previously ignored. But even more importantly, they give us a new way of looking at religion—not only its suppressions and prohibitions, its capacity to produce transgressions, but also its possibilities for freedom and liberation.

It is necessary to link the issues of gender and orientation to broader considerations of sex and the body. As feminist scholars have noted, the suppression of women within patriarchal religions has much to do with a long-standing connection between women, the body, and sex. Women are often thought to be inextricably tied to the material, embodied world, carnal desires, and the processes of reproduction. Because the goal of many traditions is to escape this realm and achieve some higher spiritual state, women and what they supposedly represent are denigrated. At the same time, precisely *because* women are associated with the power of reproduction and creation of life, their sexuality—and human sexuality in general—is an object of considerable attention in patriarchal traditions, as something that needs to be carefully managed and controlled.

By the same token, homosexuality has often been defined in terms of sexual desire and very specific sexual acts—which were of course forbidden as unnatural or in defiance of divine will. Not only were these acts representative of a lack of mastery over one's base impulses, but they also went against expectations about the way that sexuality should be expressed. In traditional Christian discourse, for example, the purpose of sex was procreation, so sexual activity that exceeded that purpose was frowned upon, even between married men and women. Homosexuality— especially between men—was therefore sinful and misdirected on a number of levels. And yet, once again, such expressions of sexuality, along with many other supposedly deviant forms, were a consistent preoccupation—even obsession—in the traditional, patriarchal setting.

As we found in discussing gender, most scholars in the history of the field either suppressed or distorted sex and the body in their work.[11] Religion was about the "higher realities": beliefs, texts, interior experience, spiritual entities, and conceptual abstractions (e.g., "the sacred," or "ultimate concern"). And if sexuality was on the agenda, it was often used to cast aspersions on the supposedly sordid practices of others. Recent scholarship has addressed these tendencies by recovering sex as an essential topic.[12] As we have noted, religion has played a major role in constructing sexuality. We need to understand the way that scriptures, institutions, and authorities dictate social and personal conduct surrounding sex—for example, who can have sex with whom and for what purpose, and what behaviors are encouraged, discouraged, or prohibited. At another level, sexuality is another vital aspect of the symbolic and conceptual imagination—the sexual identity and activities of divine figures and progenitors of the tradition, and also grander philosophical schemes: the notion, for example, that all of creation was the product of a primordial sexual act, or that sex represents the union and balance between the masculine and feminine energies that drive the universe.

Examination of sex and sexuality is, in turn, closely related to rethinking the importance of the body.[13] Especially when we study it in academic setting, it is easy to focus on the intellectual or emotional aspects of religious life—the beliefs, doctrines, and feelings that accompany it—but in doing so, we tend to leave aside its embodied component. The only way to be in the world is to be in a body, and religious traditions always have something to say about it: what it really is, but also how to manage, cure, shape, adorn, or move with it. As William R. LaFleur has noted, "Religious ideas and functions have usually tended to come strongly to the fore when it was thought that a rationale was needed for accepting certain bodily conditions as necessary and 'given' or, alternatively, when it was assumed that an existing body might be altered."[14]

Rituals, of course, are most often embodied practices, so some recent scholars direct our attention not only to what a practice means but also to how it is performed, how it is experienced as a bodily event. In addition, religious traditions present many fascinating theories about the body and its true nature, linking its subtle energies to those of cosmos, and suggesting that we can discover the connection through meditative practice. The imagery of the body has also proven useful in describing and charting out the world—conceiving all of creation, for example, as the body of God/a god, constructing temples after the shape of our bodily form, or marking off sacred spaces as locations where a divinity made contact with our plane of existence. Finally, new frontiers in the field are linking physiology to religious belief and emotions—religion can play a big role in our conception of the body, but it is also inevitable that the body and its workings are formative of religion.[15]

While sexuality and the body were not foremost on the mind of most of our classic theorists, contemporary researchers have begun to fill this gap. To leave aside sex and the body simply seems prudish, outdated, and incomplete. And the broader struggle for acceptance and recognition by LGBTQ people has also pushed this issue, this experience, onto the agenda. So we must consider these questions: *What does any given tradition or community have to say about sex? How is it regulated or imagined, and where does it break through in unexpected ways? How is the body conceived? Is being embodied a distinctive way of experiencing the world religiously? What is the normative concept of sexuality and orientation in the religious tradition or community? Do LGBTQ people have a place in it, and what is their experience?*

## Race and Ethnicity

Another limitation within the study of religion up until the last few decades has been its limited perspective on matters of race and ethnicity. Once again, the membership of those in the field might have had something to do with this failing. While scholars from many nations have engaged in the academic study of religion, it has remained a largely European and American enterprise, and until recently, people of color have been severely under-represented within it—or simply absent. Many contemporary theorists have argued that the white, Euro-American assumptions that stand behind the field have severely narrowed our understanding of the rich global, multicultural tapestry of religious life and expression.[16]

Race and ethnicity are complicated concepts, but scholars have tried to sort things out by working in two different directions. First, they argue that it is essential to focus on racial and ethnic communities to understand the ways in which they experience, re-imagine, and make religions their own. We might reflect, for example, on the distinctiveness of Christianity as practiced and understood within African-American communities. It would be worth engaging in comparative analysis: think about comparing Irish Catholicism and, say, Catholicism in Latin America, Methodism in the United States and in Korea, evangelical Protestantism in America and in Africa, the Nation of Islam in America and global Islam in other regions. Buddhism and Islam, like Christianity, are tremendously widespread traditions that have a presence in a wide variety of cultures and peoples. And then there is the multiplicity of indigenous or tribal religions that are inextricably tied to group history and memory. These are just some examples of a first layer of analysis: in researching topics like these, we discern a remarkable diversity of religious expression, the product of the interplay between religion and other significant forms of identity.

This kind of inquiry inevitably leads to another step. Scholars have shown that religious sensibilities have the power to shape and supplement a culture's concepts of race and ethnicity; in fact, as Craig Prentiss notes, "any account of the social construction of race and ethnicity will be incomplete if it fails to consider the influence of religious traditions and narratives."[17] So, for example, it seems that Christianity (or certain interpretations of it) have impacted what it means to be "black" or "white" in America. What about the complex example of Judaism, within which religion and ethnicity are so closely connected—but can also seemingly be separated (as in being "culturally Jewish")? In India, many Hindus espouse the global, universal message of their tradition, but also suggest that being a Hindu is synonymous with citizenship and membership in their nation. This seems to mean that one cannot be an Indian without being a Hindu—which is a problematic message for the hundreds of millions of Indian citizens who are Muslims, Sikhs, Jains, Buddhists, Parsis, or Christians.

There is of course a dark side to this investigation, when we confront the fact that what we call "religion" has all too often justified and promoted discrimination and persecution. Texts, such as the Bible or the Hindu Vedas, contain passages that distinguish between peoples and nations, identifying those who properly (and natively) belong to the community or tradition, and those who are outsiders. These schemes have often been interpreted as the basis of racialist and ethnocentric schemes that reinforce the idea that one group is authoritative, sacred, and holy, while others are inferior or even demonic. The history of anti-semitism is another sad testament to this reality. European anti-semitism originally received much of its justification and rationale from Christian theology, which branded Jews "Christ killers" who must be kept lowly to punish their stubbornness and ultimately force them to bear witness to the error of not accepting Jesus as their messiah, the son of God. This set of beliefs provided cover for vicious treatment of Jews for centuries.

While these forms of analysis emphasize differences and divisions, we should also note that religions often theorize race and ethnicity in a way that attempts to transcend boundaries. The differences between people that cause so much strife and conflict just do not matter or are illusory, according to this message. Early Christian texts tell us that in Christ, Jew and Gentile are the same: salvation is open to all. The Qur'an embraces all human beings, regardless of culture or skin color—one must only submit to Allah, and in doing so, the Muslim becomes a member of the global Islamic community. The Buddha resisted the heavily racialized caste system of ancient Vedic culture, and he opened the path of liberation to anyone who was willing to take it up. While religions have often reinforced hierarchy and division, they also have strong universalist tendencies that open up the possibility of belonging, commonality, and deliverance to anyone, regardless of culture, nation, or physiological features.

As is the case with gender and sexuality, focusing on the intersections between race, ethnicity, and religion gets us thinking about identity, or the multiple, intersecting identities that constitute the worldview of an individual or community. If we are to understand our fellow human beings, our study must take account of these multiple dimensions. *How has the white, Euro-American identity of the field affected the way it understands and investigates religious phenomena? How does an individual or community's racial and/or ethnic identity affect its interpretation and expression of its religious tradition? How has religion affected our concepts of race and ethnicity? In what ways does religion promote racial and ethnic differences, and in what ways does it attempt to overcome these differences?*

## Globalization, Migration, and Diaspora

Taking better account of diversity within the academic study of religion has become something of an imperative in recent decades for both ethical and methodological reasons. For one thing, it seems simply wrong for scholars to suppress certain groups and voices for no apparent reason—or, worse, out of bigotry and prejudice. At the same time, to leave large swaths of the subject matter unacknowledged or under-examined—for example, women's religious experience—is methodologically suspect: how can a field claim to treat its subject matter adequately if significant aspects of it are not on the research agenda?

It could also be argued that the recent drive to attend to the full range of human diversity in religious studies—and, indeed, the ascendancy of the field itself—simply mirrors what's happening in the world around us: an unprecedented, rapidly expanding consciousness of different kinds of people. In other words, this discipline—just like everything else—has been affected and enabled by *globalization*. Globalization is another term whose meaning is much debated,[18] but in general, it refers to the acceleration of worldwide exchange, mobility, and connectivity that has occurred in the last few decades. Globalization can be taken as another term for the spread of dominant Western political, economic, and cultural systems, for which colonialism and the rise of Euro-American power set the stage. But it also refers to the relative ease with which people, goods, and information now flow in all directions, from region to region, city to city, continent to continent, culture to culture. Hence, the term refers to the realities behind an unprecedented global outlook, realities that are played out within the powerful ground rules of modernity, but which also permit the expression, influence, and pushback of diverse voices that in earlier times were rarely heard beyond the confines of their region, city, village, or home.

The conventional wisdom tells us that globalization and religion are opposing forces. According to this reading, globalization carries with it many of the features of secular societies: capitalism, advertising, consumerism, corporations, democracy, church/state separation, technology, and liberalization of social morality and roles. Thus globalization would seem to threaten the distinctiveness of cultural and religious identities. Religion is a difference that many of our fellow human beings hold onto for dear life, and yet globalization may be forcing it to standardize, as more and more people make accommodations within the larger forces that are at work.

To an extent, this description is correct, but some scholars have also urged us to take a more nuanced view. They have reminded us, for example, that Christianity has accompanied the spread of European and American extension of power and influence; as sociologist of religion Bryan Turner has noted, "'the world religions' have been globalizing forces long before the modern period."[19] We also know that religion has responded to secularization and globalization, at times quite vigorously: it is not simply surrendering as a result of these seemingly overwhelming forces. In addition, perhaps most interesting is the fact that in many cases the globalized situation has actually opened up the playing field for a variety of religious movements, allowing them to spread more widely and to become more influential on global culture and international politics.[20]

Globalization is, after all, about flows of people and increased levels of interconnection; as Mark Juergensmeyer has put it, "Today it seems that almost everyone is everywhere."[21] So more and more frequently we witness religious situations that are an intricate mixture of "crossing and dwelling."[22] Migrants have always had a distinctive experience as they wrestle with identity and belonging within their adopted culture. Should they assimilate, stay withdrawn within their own community, or try to find some kind of compromise in between? Religion has often been a major factor in determining which path an immigrant community takes. Residing in a place dominated by a tradition other than one's own can present a lot of challenges, especially if individuals and groups are subject to negative treatment or persecution. But a diverse, pluralist environment can be just as tricky: living in the midst of a wide range of identities and outlooks comes with its own decisions and difficulties.

In the new, globalized circumstance, heightened connectivity also allows migrants to maintain close contact with their homeland, even if they are deeply committed to making a life in the new place. This experience can be complicated. After all, where is home? In the country of one's origin, where most of the family still resides, where one's culture is pervasive, where the most significant sacred places and people are located? Or perhaps home is in the new land by necessity, but with a heavy layer of reluctance and nostalgia. *Diaspora* communities maintain symbolic, historical, and psychological ties to the homeland, while often acknowledging that there is no going back. The Jewish tradition, for example, is thoroughly constituted by this experience, the sense that since the archetypal "diaspora" of the first-century CE, in which the Romans destroyed the temple in Jerusalem and scattered the Jewish people across Europe, Jews have simply not been at home—they have instead lived in minority communities all over the globe. This experience is shared by many diasporic peoples—Africans, Latin Americans, Southeast Asians, among others—who have been driven, for a variety of reasons, to move on and away. Globalization has only accelerated and made more frequent the occurrence of diaspora.[23]

So analysis of the relationship between religion and globalizing forces continues to unfold. At stake are fascinating matters of description and prediction, which overlap significantly with our work in the field. This will become all the more clear as we proceed with discussion of new religions, "New Age" spirituality, fundamentalism, liberationist theologies, and religious violence, below. There is no way to understand these phenomena without grappling with globalization, but before moving on, we should keep some framing questions in mind: *What exactly is globalization? How does it intersect with religion (and the academic study of religion)? How have religious traditions been "global" in the past, and how is globalization affecting their development today? What is the unique experience of immigrant, migrant, refugee, and diasporic individuals, and how does that experience intersect with their religious commitments and identity?*

# Religion in Transformation: New Movements and Trends

It could be said that religions are nothing without the changes they undergo. Traditions attempt to adhere to basic principles and maintain continuity, but they also change course and evolve. Such transformation is often gradual, maybe even imperceptible to insiders, but it can also be radical and sudden. The contemporary study of religion is sensitive to both gradual change and also rapid innovation as it keeps pace with subject matter that is in a constant state of flux.

As we just indicated, globalization is a major change-agent in our world; it intersects with a wide variety of developments and trends, from large to small, from global to regional to local. In Chapter 1 we already took note of contemporary discussions about where religion in general is headed—whether its influence was increasing or decreasing—and we found that, as always, this question is complex. In some contexts, in Western Europe and to a certain extent the United States, for example, adherence to institutional religion is declining, and the prevalence of religious belief is becoming less widespread. And yet, in the bigger global picture, long-standing traditions have maintained their hold and in some cases seem to be resurgent and more visible than ever. Change is an inevitable feature of religion, but there is no one simple way to characterize its trends—we must be ready to see it as the complex, multiple-layered reality that it is.

Part of this complexity comes from the fact that religious communities have always had a habit of transforming as a result of doctrinal disagreements, political disputes, reform movements, and the force of external events. Traditions split and splinter, and they divide into major branches and smaller sects. They also spin off even smaller groups that tend to drop out of the mainstream and establish isolated, communal, counter-cultural lifestyles, often prompted by the teachings of a charismatic leader. Such groups are known as "cults" in the wider culture, but scholars now prefer to call them "New Religious Movements," or NRMs for short.[24]

In Chapters 1 and 2, we already considered the challenges that these small but potent groups pose. For one thing, they don't fit within our usual understanding of the family of "world religions." In fact, their tense relationship with both well-established traditions and secular society is often what defines them. NRMs also tend to be syncretistic: they borrow and pick and choose and piece together a new vision. As NRM scholar Susan J. Palmer has noted, "I encounter oddly coherent worldviews constructed higgledy-piggledy out of the most incongruous elements: songs of Solomon, UFO lore, electric bulbs, biofeedback machines, gnostic creation myths—all welded into one seamless syncretism."[25] Most provocative, perhaps, is the intense devotion that the followers of these movements display, a commitment that has, on occasion, led to confrontation, murder, and group suicide.

For these and many other reasons, in analyzing groups such as Jim Jones's People's Temple, the Branch Davidians at Waco, Aum Shinrikyo (Japan), the International Society for Krishna Consciousness (ISKCON, i.e., the Hare Krishnas), the Nation of Islam, Falun Gong (China), or Scientology, we must take full advantage of our theoretical tools to bring these cases into focus. Despite its nonconformity and initial strangeness, we should recall that the "New Religious Movement" of today has the potential to become the "world religion" of tomorrow, and thus it is well worth our careful attention. "Each 'cult' is a mini-culture, a protocivilization," Susan J. Palmer explains, "a baby religion."[26]

In connection with the study of NRMs, we should again bring to mind the widespread outlook that also puts many of our theoretical models to the test: "spirituality," or the somewhat more specific, "alternative" or "New Age spirituality."[27] In Chapter 1 we alluded to "seekers" or "nones" (when asked about religious affiliation, they say "none"), and noted that in the United States in particular, it is common to find people who say that they are "spiritual," not "religious," meaning that for them, this issue is a matter of individual choice and should be decoupled from institutions like the Church. Spiritual seekers often assemble their own beliefs and practices, constructing a therapeutic worldview that is subject to adjustment as the individual changes. Life is, after all, a journey—or so the New Age mantra tells us.

Given the prevalence of this ethos, students of religion are called upon to analyze and explain it, despite the fact that "its opacity admits too much but precludes too little."[28] Following the general trend of modern society, personal choice and individual experience have perhaps moved to the center. This orientation would appear quite strange to many people across the globe, because it privatizes the "spiritual" life, makes the variety of religions into a marketplace for individuals to choose from, and leaves aside binding obligations. Thus thinking about "spirituality" renews broader questions about definitions and the "world religions" scheme. If spiritual movements don't fit within accepted paradigms for categorization, maybe this is a problem with the accepted paradigms—and not with this widespread and empirically significant phenomenon.[29]

While NRMs, syncretistic worldviews, and spiritual seekers tend to chart out innovative, nontraditional territory, others strive to bring traditions back to their foundations. *Fundamentalism* is yet another commonly used and much debated term, but in general, it points to movements that engage in a vigorous response to a perceived modern assault on their communities, urging a return to the absolute "fundamentals" of the tradition. For example, the Christian fundamentalist[30] may insist on a literalist interpretation of the Bible, direct encounter with the saving power of Jesus Christ, strict adherence to the example of what they imagine Jesus himself would do, expectation of Christ's apocalyptic return, and resistance to the findings of science (e.g., evolution). In the Jewish tradition, a fundamentalist might urge recognition of the Torah as the direct language of God, rigid conformity to religious law, in some cases (among the ultra-orthodox) strict separation from non-Jewish society, and, again, in some cases, fervent devotion to the Jewish state, Israel. Hindu fundamentalists may cite the sole authority of the Vedas, insist on the notion of India as a purely Hindu state, and espouse the principle of Aryan/Indian identity. And in Islam, some factions attempt to enforce narrow interpretation of shari'ah (Muslim law) based directly on Qur'anic injunctions, hold up the original community of the prophet Muhammad as a model for contemporary life, and enforce a strongly authoritarian structure of leadership and community. As scholars have discovered, there are multiple variables that attach to what we now call fundamentalism, including its vigorous response to secularism, selective use of tradition and scriptures, moral absolutism, apocalyptic notions, exclusive membership, authoritarian social structures, and rigid behavioral expectations.[31] If anything ties it all together, it is perhaps the idea that the tradition is threatened and embattled, and that a return to a foundational set of beliefs or epoch is necessary. The authority of these fundamentals is thought to well exceed that of other religions, and especially secular, nonreligious institutions and forms of life.

While traditional elements—texts, founders, law, ritual, experience, and identity—are vital in these movements, it should be reiterated that their existence is intimately connected with modern, contemporary life. We might say that "fundamentalists" have always been around, that is, groups who are deeply committed to the basic principles of their tradition. Practically everyone in premodern Europe, for example, was a "fundamentalist" by contemporary standards. But contemporary fundamentalist movements are not simply throwbacks to some earlier era; they have a uniquely modern identity and standing. For example, many scholars have argued that these groups see themselves as embattled, marginalized, or even oppressed by their wider cultures, and so their very existence is owed to this perspective. Fundamentalists also take a strong, visible stand on issues that were simply not part of their history (e.g., abortion, climate change, genetic science, evolutionary theory, etc.), and they are often eager to use technology and the media to connect with their followers and get their message across. Despite its rhetoric, fundamentalism is very much a contemporary phenomenon.[32]

While fundamentalism is highly visible and draws a great deal of attention, it is of course not the only religious response to the challenges of contemporary life, nor even the most prevalent one. In contrast, many communities and individuals have opted to embrace key aspects of secular worldviews, rather than rejecting them wholesale. This trend has led practitioners to greater acceptance of science, reason, universal human rights, societal justice, and religious tolerance, and thus also to critique and reform of aspects of their own tradition that are thought to be archaic or discriminatory, while *also* recalling the fact that many of the values that many of us now hold dear (e.g., human rights) actually have religious origins.[33]

Given this complexity, the move toward *liberalization* has taken many different forms, in the full variety of traditions.[34] Reform Judaism, for example, resists gender segregation and inequality and often preaches acceptance of gays and lesbians. It resists the strict moral and ritual distinction between Jews and non-Jews, accepts the value and dignity of other religious traditions, and grants wide latitude to individual communities to interpret their Jewish religious and cultural identity as they see fit, by means of dialogue among members, with reference to the tradition.[35] Within Catholicism, the Second Vatican Council (1962–65) introduced a variety of liberalizing reforms, including delivery of the mass not in Latin, but in the native language of the parishioners; greater tolerance of other religious traditions and elimination of ancient anti-Semitic doctrines; acceptance of basic distinctions between church and state power; and relaxation of a variety of moral and ritual strictures.[36] In a way, Vatican II opened the door for *liberationist* movements, particularly in Latin and South America, which connected the impulse of secular leftist politics — promoting social and economic justice, especially among the poor and oppressed—with the essence of the Christian message. In another prominent example, the Dalai Lama is the head of a very traditional branch of Buddhism, and yet he is very interested in making connections between science and Buddhist teachings. He has articulated concerns about climate change and the environment, advocates for dialogue between religions, and promotes gender equality, going so far as to suggest that his next reincarnation—the next Dalai Lama—might be a woman from outside Tibet or India.

In all these examples—and in the lives of a multitude of believers—the moral force of doctrines that are generally thought to be secular has led to the need for change and reform. But, as we noted above, religions have always been subject to transformation in response to both internal and external pressures. Thinking about NRMs, spirituality, fundamentalism, and liberalizing movements in the frame of globalization reminds us about the dynamism of our topic: this is a moving target, so our theories and approaches need to be mobile enough to capture it, starting with the right questions: *How should we study and understand New Religious Movements? What theoretical tools will best help us to understand these new developments on the religious landscape? What about the idea of being "spiritual, not religious"? How should we explain the emergence of this distinction? Is it a good starting point for the interpretation of religion? In studying a religious community or its members, where does it locate itself in relation to secularism and the forces of globalization? How should we understand and analyze the spectrum of these responses, ranging from fundamentalist to liberalizing? What, in general, are the factors that generate religious change?*

## Religious Violence (and Peace)

When we reflected on the question "Why study religion today?" in the opening chapter of this book, one of the most immediate answers was the pressing need to understand religious conflict and violence. There is no denying the fact that religion has become linked to violent struggle in public discourse—and for good reason, because this link, while complex, is quite real. As we noted, Islamic terrorism is the example that leaps to most people's minds, but current scholarship tempers this fixation by reminding us that no tradition is innocent: not Christianity, with its injunction to "turn the other cheek"; not Judaism, with its emphasis on ethics and law; not Hinduism, with its tolerant conception of diversity in unity; not even Buddhism, with its emphasis on *ahimsa*, or "refraining from harm." So how is it that religions turn violent?[37]

Obviously there is no universal, clear-cut answer to this question. Some authors have argued that religion—or particular religions—are inherently violent by nature.[38] Others counter that they are essentially peaceful; it is other factors, such as oppression, poverty, injustice, or our biological nature that leads them to the dark side, or it is a small minority of fanatics who have "hijacked" a tradition for their own nefarious, self-serving purposes. Of course, as always, the truth probably resides somewhere in between, "[f]or religion is neither inherently peaceful, nor does it automatically and inevitably lead to conflict."[39] On the one hand, as John D. Carlson has noted, "*any* single representation [of "true" religion being essentially peaceful] risks displacing the many other complex, multivalent pieces made up of innumerable actors, movements, texts, discourses, and institutions—and which, together, form no overarching montage or composite of 'authentic religion.'"[40] So it is very difficult—if not impossible—to isolate some core that is peaceful, to which war and violence are merely appendages. Here we once again cross paths with the question of definition and the danger of essentialism. To say that religion is essentially peaceful is to presuppose an understanding of its essence—and as we have seen in the pages of this book, that is a highly debatable move.

But the same goes for the claim that religion is inherently violent. As a number of scholars have argued—perhaps most notably William Cavanaugh—the very idea of "religious violence" depends on a prior distinction between "the secular," which is assumed to be the harbinger of peace and progress, and "the religious," which is violent and retrograde. Cavanaugh goes so far as to call "religious violence" a "myth," identifies the concept as a tool for propping up the superiority of "the West" in contrast with the "irrational Other" (e.g., Islam),[41] and explains that reality—which includes constant intermingling of "secular" and "religious" violence—is far more complex than is generally assumed. As Cavanaugh and many others have suggested, we cannot shy away from forces and precedents within traditions that set the stage for hostility, whether on a grand or an intimate scale. But careful scholarship also reminds us that it usually takes a combination of factors to push individuals and communities over the edge. To this extent, fixating on religion as a singular cause of a aggressive act or campaign of terror is an interpretive mistake—but so is giving it a free pass, because of some idyllic essence.

There is a difference, however, between wishful thinking and acknowledging that religions also contain resources for peaceful solutions and social progress. Perhaps we should invert the question that we posed above—"How is it that religions turn violent?"—and ask, "How is it that religions turn peaceful?" While it is indeed naïve to say that all traditions are essentially nonviolent, they have instituted basic precepts that guide, restrict, and often prohibit war and violence, both on the individual and communal level. Communities across the globe have strongly endorsed a commitment to basic rights and the fundamental dignity and commonality of all humanity, drawing upon their own precedents in scripture, law, and practice. In addition, many great movements opposing war, oppression, discrimination, and socially or politically sanctioned brutality have been religiously inspired. Here we need only think of figures such as Mahatma Gandhi in India, Martin Luther King in the United States, Archbishop Desmond Tutu in South Africa, and Aung San Suu Kyi in Myanmar/Burma. With so much attention to conflict and bloodshed in our day and age, it is important to keep this counter-balance in mind: many religious people live an existence that is relatively free of aggression, anger, or offense. And their worldviews have often contributed to keeping the peace.[42]

With this balanced perspective in place, you will be in a good position to start working on questions that are very much on the cutting edge in the field: *Why does religious violence happen? Is there such a thing as "religious violence"? Do religions have a tendency toward violence? Toward peace? Do certain religious traditions (or particular interpretations of them) have more potential for giving rise to violence? How have religions contributed to the cause of peace, justice, and reconciliation?*

## Science: Cosmology, Evolution, Medicine, and the Environment

In the standard picture, religious and scientific worldviews have been conceived as contrary to each other: religion is based on nonrational faith in the unseen, whereas science relies on reason and empirical method. It is quite true that the ascendancy of the natural sciences and speed of technological innovation have challenged traditionalist views, sometimes shaking them to the core and producing a deep rift between the two "*magisteria*" (domains) of religion and science, as the biologist Stephen Jay Gould called them. At the same time, the persistence of long-standing beliefs and practices has often perplexed and disturbed scientifically minded observers. A number of them in our day and age have expressed this frustration, renewing predictions of (and hopes for) religion's demise.[43]

While there is no denying these tensions, contemporary scholars have shown that the relationship between religion and science has been more complicated than is commonly assumed. As Ian Barbour has argued, for example, it has taken four different forms: conflict, independence (seeing religion and science as two independent, radically different arenas), dialogue (comparison between ideas and findings), and integration (active synthesis of religious and scientific perspectives).[44] Barbour provides us with an interesting framework for examining the data: while the *conflicts* are highly visible, it is just as common to discover more constructive or positive forms of integration, or a live-and-let-live form of indifference. We should be open to these nuances, rather than always assuming antagonism. Many religious people are interested and invested in science, and many scientists hold religious beliefs.[45] As always, the situation is complex.

Taking another step forward, contemporary scientific approaches, particularly cognitive neuroscience and evolutionary psychology, are shedding new light on the origins and persistence of religious adherence—and not necessarily with the purpose of simply explaining it away. It is undeniable that one of the biggest conflicts between traditional worldviews and modern science has arisen around *cosmology* and *evolution*. Most religious traditions have their own mythic conceptions of the beginnings of the cosmos, the creation of our world, and the origin of life on earth. As greats such as Albert Einstein and Carl Sagan pointed out, these speculations have something in common with science: they arise from a sense of wonder and curiosity in the face of the vastness of our cosmic order. But this experience can obviously lead in very different directions. The first chapter of Genesis, for example, presents a singular, linear narrative of God's creation in six days that has been placed in historical time by some interpreters, resulting in the conclusion that the world was created some 6,000–7,000 years ago. Many Christians still adhere to this notion; there is in fact a museum devoted to it.[46] Scientists present overwhelming physical evidence to the contrary, dating our world at four or five billion years old, tracing the universe back to over thirteen billion years old, and placing the emergence of *Homo sapiens* at about 200,000 years ago. Needless to say, at least on the face of it, there seems to be little room for compromise between these two positions.

The controversy gets even more tangled when we turn to the origins of life on earth. Philosophers and theologians have employed the apparent design of the world, and particularly the design of biological entities within it, to support belief in the existence of a single intelligent designer, that is, God. In a way, science comes to the aid of this argument. How could something as intricate as the human eye, for example, be a random shot in the dark? Didn't someone or something have to craft it, intentionally? Doesn't science continue to show us the ingenuity at work behind such features of the organic world? In the wake of the evolutionary theory proposed by Charles Darwin (1809–82), scientists have argued that, in fact, the eye came from a process of randomness and selection that extended over hundreds of millions of years. There was no divine blueprint for organisms, only a long history of adaptations that were slowly and gradually selected to make survival more likely. Again, the evidence in support of this theory is overwhelming, yet it flatly contradicts a central belief, held by many: human beings were made by and in the image of God. And it also goes directly against the idea that human beings were created within the last few thousand years.[47]

This is not the right place to try to adjudicate these debates, yet they do provide the backdrop for cutting-edge approaches in the academic study of religion. Religion, some scholars have argued, was a product (or by-product) of evolutionary adaptation, and on a closely related note, they suggest that "many aspects of religion are constrained to a certain extent by the normal functioning of the cognitive system."[48] Belief in the existence of supernatural beings, for example, may be an extension of our keen (and necessary) ability to pick up on threats in the natural environment and to be hypersensitive to the forces behind them, which are often hidden. Other theories suggest that rituals and story-telling promoted social cohesion, which was vital to human survival, or that the emergence of religious sensibilities was closely linked to the development of complex language abilities, which also gave us an evolutionary advantage. Researchers have additionally proposed that belief in God/gods developed in response to our need to maintain an ordered, meaningful experience of the world, which was necessary for our well-being and thus our survival. While theories such as these do call into question the views of most insiders—and also a more traditional version of religious studies—they also suggest that religious realities are enmeshed with the kinds of physical beings that we have become. As a consequence, this approach gives us scientifically grounded way of understanding and explaining religion's persistence, even in the face of deep skepticism and social change.

The relationship between religion and medical science is another, related issue. As the previous discussion of evolution suggests, the naturalistic worldview promoted by science sees us primarily as a material, biological entity. Thus the treatment of sickness, injury, and suffering is a matter of addressing physiological processes via medical scientific practices. Historically speaking, most traditional worldviews have seen things quite differently, explaining our woes in mythic terms (e.g., as the product of supernatural forces), as a product of moral failings (e.g., the result of sin), or in accordance with metaphysical schemes (e.g., an imbalance of subtle energies). The differences between religious and naturalistic perspectives have led to significant and highly visible conflicts, in recent decades: the abortion, stem-cell, and euthanasia debates are good examples. Genetic therapy is another challenging prospect, because for some it crosses into territory that should be off-limits: the design, manipulation, and perhaps even creation of human existence. At the same time, some believers reject even the most basic treatments because of their faith commitments; meanwhile many practitioners reject mainstream medicine in favor of other alternative schemes for health and healing.

And yet, despite these basic conflicts, as we found in discussing religion and science and general, the interaction between medicine and religious worldviews continues to be complex. Gary B. Ferngren has noted that the relation between religion and medicine takes a number of forms, with religion subsuming medicine in some cases, medicine subsuming religion in others, and a range of possibilities in between, including both dialogue and maintaining clear boundaries between the two spheres.[49] Once again, the big cultural debates might grab our attention, but careful analysis reveals a tricky and intricate relationship between religion and healing—thus it's a fascinating area to explore.

Before moving on, we should consider one other, extremely pressing area of contemporary research in the field that is closely related to the interaction between religious and scientific worldviews, namely the environment. As we saw in the discussion of gender, race, and sexuality earlier in this chapter, broader social and political movements have pushed the environment, ecology, and nature onto the agenda of the academic study of religion in recent decades. The threat of environmental degradation—pollution, species extinction, and climate change—has fueled this subfield. But familiar debates have emerged. Is it the job of the scholar of religion and the environment to attempt to promote change, to criticize elements of religious traditions that have harmed the natural world and to encourage positive ideas and practices? Or should this remain a more neutral, analytical project, where we aim to understand and interpret this connection, without necessarily taking a position?

Debate about these questions continues, but even if we limit the scope of our exploration to description and analysis, we see the potential of this subfield. A productive approach to exploring any given tradition is examining its relationship with and impact on nature. For example, scholars have highlighted the basic assumption that in Genesis, God created man and woman in his image and gave humanity dominion over all of creation. This separation of both God and humankind from nature, one could argue, has been a premise for exploiting it. Some ecologically minded scholars also point out that the appearance of the "Father God," who is distant from and in some sense opposed to nature, suppressed a matriarchal tradition that privileged the feminine principle: "Mother Earth" or "Gaia." In theory, this ancient tradition was much more respectful of the earth because it was conceived to be divine. As a rejoinder to these critiques, interpreters point out that Bible also inserts an element of responsibility: nature is everywhere in its stories and teachings, and from the beginning, God took great pride in his creation and made humankind its responsible steward. The modern, industrialized West, one might suggest, has failed in upholding that duty: it is the secular worldview that has caused the most dramatic problems, not the religious.

Reaching beyond biblical traditions, we find that situating religious belief and practice in relation to nature continues to yield some interesting results. How would we look at the environment differently, for example, if God/the gods were somehow within it, and not outside it? Indigenous traditions, including many Native American traditions, often uphold this belief, and Neo-paganism is a contemporary movement that has attempted to revive a more positive, intimate human relationship with the natural world. In some of the major "world religions" too, we discover a commitment to the interconnectedness of all things, and thus, in Hinduism and Buddhism, for example, all life is thought to be part of the same cycle of birth and re-birth. As a result, Hindus and Buddhists are encouraged to practice *ahimsa*, or "refraining from harm" to all sentient beings. In addition, some forms of Taoism see nature as the quintessential model for following the true Way (Tao) that operates behind all things;

nature is the absolute authority, not scriptures, not humans, not gods.[50] This is not to say that all practitioners of these traditions (and others like them) are "environmentally conscious," but exploring these views—and the myths and practices that are related to them—gives us a valuable perspective on our subject matter. And it also gives us some additional insight on an issue that is—for very good reason—at the forefront of our cultural and political consciousness.[51]

Even this quick survey should give you a sense of the huge territory that is opened up by considering the connections between science and religion. These two spheres of experience and knowledge have pervaded the lives, in one way or another, of every human being, and they have a complex historical relationship with each other. In our day and age, science is also shedding new light on religious phenomena, leading to significant shifts in the field. Research will continue to unfold, guided by a pressing set of questions: *What is the historical relationship between religions and science? How have they influenced each other? How do evolutionary theory and cognitive science change our approach to the study of religion? Where have religious traditions and medicine intersected, and where are the conflicts? How does any given tradition conceive of nature in its myths, scriptures, and beliefs? What natural symbols are present? Is nature something to be protected, suppressed, or disregarded? How do religions relate to the contemporary environmental crisis?*

## Religion's Expressions: Material Culture, Art, Media, and Online

Once again recalling our classic theorists from Chapters 3 and 4, we had numerous opportunities to reflect on the symbolic, material, and aesthetic components of religious life. Durkheim, for example, analyzed the power of sacred totems that represent group identity, and he found that tribe members adorn themselves and their surroundings with these emblems and often put them at the center of ritual practices. Geertz's first step in his famous definition was to say that religion is "a system of symbols," which often take material form in the lives of practitioners, like a cross that hangs around a Christian's neck. Freud and Jung also devoted considerable attention to symbols because they refer to deep, often unspoken realities that stand behind the conscious realm. Eliade showed us that the sacred manifests itself in symbols that are closely linked to myth and ritual; in the modalities of time and space, these manifestations take shape within a scale from the microcosmic to the grand, from, for example, the household shrine to the massive cathedral. Finally, Paul Tillich's "method of correlation" led him to explore the link between symbols, art, and the foundation of belief and practice, "ultimate concern."

This list could easily go on as we recall the work of foundational authors in the field, and yet, contemporary scholars have offered important updates and correctives. For example, as we have noted on a number of occasions, the field as a whole has tended to emphasize beliefs, or the intellectual content behind religiosity, at the expense of *material culture*.[52] Even the classic notion of a *symbol* generally suggests that objects are really about something else, some more profound *idea* or *meaning*. But as the saying (falsely attributed to Freud) goes, "Sometimes a cigar is just a cigar"—or if this is a bit too simplistic, sometimes a cigar is just about smoking it. The material dimension of religion includes the objects associated with ritual practice and everyday life, and their connection with some deep existential meaning or central doctrine is not always dramatic, nor is it always apparent. Examples of these objects are innumerable: a postcard depicting the Hindu god Ganesh on the dashboard of a taxi; the mezuzah on the doorframe marking a Jewish home; the beads around the wrist of an Catholic, Muslim, or Buddhist; the white ihram garment donned by Muslims undertaking the hajj; the book of scripture itself, the Bible, the Qur'an, the Torah scroll; the plastic, illuminated manger scene in an American front yard; or a chunk of marble with the Ten Commandments inscribed on it, in front of city hall. And so on. As Richard Carp has noted, "*Material religion* is everything perceptible that is part of a religious tradition."[53]

Many scholars find this dimension the most interesting, because these objects are intimate and collective treasures. For present purposes, maybe what's most intriguing is the challenge they pose to our thinking about theorizing the content of religion. As Matthew Engelke observes, "All religion is material religion . . . But the difficult part comes in understanding what precisely constitutes the *materiality* of material religion, what makes religious materiality either significant or religious, and according to whom."[54] For example, every year American Christians (and non-Christians, for that matter) celebrate Easter. Easter marks the most important episode in the primal myth of the Christian tradition: the death and resurrection of Jesus Christ. Yet in many communities and cultures, a parallel drama unfolds that involves eggs (boiled and dyed; plastic, containing sweets; or chocolate) and rabbits (small and large). What do these two narratives and systems of ritual practice have to do with each other?[55] Insiders will have their own various answers; some Christians embrace the kitschy trappings of material culture (the eggs and bunnies) and some reject them. Meanwhile, many non-Christians take part in the broader cultural ritual. The student of religion takes such instances as a testing ground for our theoretical approaches: what's religious here, and what is not? Or does all of this—bunnies and all—somehow fit within a synthetic whole? The same kind of questions arise within the many, various forms of religious material culture, including food, dress, dance, and music.[56]

Of course, we might wish to make some distinction between these intimate objects and "high religious art," which is designed for grand aesthetic and spiritual effect. In these cases, it can be difficult to determine whether the art serves the religion or religion serves the art. Here we include magnificent examples of religious painting, statuary, and textiles, and the monumental buildings that contain them. Think of the great European cathedrals such as Notre Dame; Michaelangelo's masterpiece on the ceiling of the Sistine Chapel; the huge Tibetan tapestries depicting mandalas, complex ritual diagrams depicting holy people and cosmic regions; or massive statues, such as the 60-foot tall depictions in stone of Jain saints in India. At the same time, the artistic dimension of religion takes other spectacular shapes, in music, such as Handel's *Messiah*, for example, or in literature, such as Dante's *Divine Comedy*. It is clear that the religious is not just an abstraction: it *takes shape* and *takes place* in a seemingly infinite variety of ways.[57]

Modern artistic production has a life of its own, and yet, as many observers have shown, it continues to be attracted to religious content, both in "high art" and popular culture. Contemporary forms of technology now mediate the religious spectacle, on both a grand and intimate scale.[58] Religious themes permeate popular forms of entertainment, including music, film, sports, and television: a survey of recent volumes on this topic reveals analysis of religion and Madonna, U2, Kanye West, Bob Dylan, *The Da Vinci Code*, *Lord of the Rings*, *Twilight*, *Star Wars*, the Red Sox, *Star Trek*, *American Idol*, *American Family*, video games, pornography, and brands such as Coca-Cola and Apple.[59]

In addition, the internet and social media have added a whole new dimension. A number of well-traveled websites cover the religion beat, offering insight, information, and analysis, including BeliefNet (beliefnet.com), CNN Belief Blog (religion.blogs.cnn.com), HuffPost Religion (huffingtonpost.com/religion/), Killing the Buddha (killingthebuddha.com), OnFaith (faithstreet.com/onfaith), Patheos (patheos.com), and Religion Dispatches (religiondispatches.org). Within religious communities, practitioners have also turned to new media to get their message out, transmit their activities, and even to engage in worship and ritual practice. In a classic example, some Hindu websites, present the image of a god and urge worshipers to take its *puja* (worship) online.[60] Christian preachers have been on American television since its inception, but now the modes of preaching, proselytizing, and fellowship building have shifted to the web, blogs, Facebook, Twitter, YouTube, Instagram, and text blasts. Virtually all religious communities that have access to the technology now have an internet and social media presence. There are even new movements that are entirely online. Is it possible that the next "world religion" will not exist in the "real world" at all, but instead will be entirely virtual?[61]

Where these new forms will go is a wide open question. At the very least, religious literacy is an absolute requirement for studying the history of art in almost any cultural context. At the same time, it also prepares us for whatever new forms of expression come our way. *How do ritual and everyday objects express the religious worldview to which they belong? How do they fit into the everyday lives and life-stories of practitioners? What is the best way to read and interpret grander examples of religious art? What religious themes can be discerned in modern art? To what extent is living a religious life similar to living an artistic life? And how do new technologies and media affect religious experience?*

As we noted at the very beginning of this book, for some observers, religion is an archaism, a collection of outmoded superstitions that come to us from the benighted past. To this extent, some would say, anyone who is devoting time to studying this subject is either simply wasting his or her time or subconsciously contributing to its continuation—unless he or she has the express purpose of analyzing it in order to get rid of it.

If the contemporary state of the field is any indication, then we must again—as we did at the beginning—call this view into question. While until recently the field followed the drift of its culture, suppressing or denigrating huge swaths of human experience, it now finds itself in a new circumstance—pluralistic, global, and mediated—that calls for ever more sophisticated theoretical and methodological approaches, building on the foundations laid by canonical theorists. Do we understand this subject better than we did several decades ago? Even if we have not unlocked all of its mysteries, it is safe to say that the academic study of religion has progressed, evolving from a field that was alloyed with the thing that it was supposed to examine, or an intellectual project that was bent on eliminating it, into an independent site of inquiry, a secure, defined space for promoting curiosity and ultimately understanding.

Which brings us back to our old friend William James, who had this to say about his passionate interest in this strange, familiar thing called religion:

> Religion, whatever it is, is a man's [or woman's] total reaction upon life, so why not say that any total reaction upon life is a religion? . . . To get at [total reactions] you must go behind the foreground of existence and reach down to that curious sense of the whole residual cosmos as an everlasting presence . . . This sense of the world's presence, appealing as it does to our peculiar individual temperament, makes us either strenuous or careless, devout or blasphemous, gloomy or exultant, about life at large; and our reaction . . . is the completest of all our answers to the question, "What is the character of this universe in which we dwell?"[62]

James thought that the foundational element of religion, its Zero Order (going back to Chapter 2), was an unseen, underlying realm (here characterized as "the whole residual cosmos as an everlasting presence") that makes itself known through an individual, prerational encounter. You now have the tools to reflect on and evaluate this "theoretical idea," to test its strengths and weaknesses and determine its utility.

But also take note of the sentiments here that are indispensable within the discipline, as we have described it. James urges you to "go behind the foreground of existence," to see what's behind appearances. That is the primary goal of theoretical literacy: to interpret this subject matter in a methodologically self-conscious way; to define, describe, explain, and predict effectively; and thus to reach a better understanding. James also brings us back to the very beginning of this book, to J. Z. Smith's proposal: "What we study when we study religion is one mode of constructing worlds of meaning, worlds within which men [and women] find themselves and in which they choose to dwell." As you have discovered, these worlds that accommodate many of our fellow human beings are endlessly fascinating, calling out for us to join James and the rest of the classic theorists we have examined with our own passionate engagement.

# Notes

1. Edward Said, *Orientalism* (New York: Vintage Books, 1979), 3.
2. See Richard King, *Orientalism and Religion: Postcolonial Theory, India and "The Mystic East"* (London and New York: Routledge, 1999).
3. See Tomoko Masuzawa, *The Invention of World Religions: Or, How European Universalism Was Preserved in the Language of Pluralism* (Chicago and London: The University of Chicago Press, 2005).
4. A challenging collection that takes a postmodern, anti-essentialist approach to the study of religion: Mark C. Taylor (ed.), *Critical Terms for Religious Studies* (Chicago and London: The University of Chicago Press, 1998).
5. For an excellent starting point for research in this area, see Ursula King (ed.), *Religion and Gender* (Oxford and Malden, MA: Blackwell Publishers, 1995). Also see Arvind Sharma (ed.), *Today's Woman in World Religions*, (Albany: State University of New York Press, 1994); Elizabeth Castelli (ed.), *Women, Gender, Religion: A Reader* (New York: Palgrave, 2001); and Darlene Juschka (ed.), *Feminism in the Study of Religion: A Reader* (London and New York: Continuum, 2001). For cutting-edge work that takes account of developments in gender studies, queer theory, and the academic study of religion, see the open access journal, *Religion and Gender*, which was launched in 2011 (www.religionandgender.org).
6. Elisabeth Schüssler Fiorenza, *In Memory of Her: A Feminist Theological Reconstruction of Christian Origins* (New York: Crossroad, 1983).
7. Lisbeth Mikaelsson, "Gendering the History of Religions," in *New Approaches to the Study of Religion, Volume 1: Regional, Critical, and Historical Approaches*, ed. Peter Antes, Armin W. Geertz, and Randi R. Warne (Berlin: Walter de Gruyter, 2004), 297.
8. A reference to Mary McClintock Fulkerson, *Changing the Subject: Women's Discourses and Feminist Theology* (Minneapolis, MN: Fortress Press, 1994).
9. See *Que(e)rying Religion: A Critical Anthology*, ed. Gary David Comstock and Susan E. Henking (London and New York: Continuum, 1997).
10. See Melissa M. Wilcox, "Outlaws or In-Laws? Queer Theory, LGBT Studies, and Religious Studies," in *LGBT Studies and Queer Theory: New Conflicts, Collaborations and Contested Terrain*, ed. Karen E. Lovaas, John P. Elia, and Gust A. Yep (Binghamton, NY: Harrington Park Press, 2006), 73–100.
11. For a discussion of sex as a descriptive category in the history of the field, see R. Marie Griffith, "Sexing Religion," in *The Cambridge Companion to Religious Studies*, ed. Robert Orsi (New York: Cambridge University Press, 2012), 338–59.

12. See Griffith, "Sexing Religion," 357. For a collection of relevant sources from a range of religious traditions, see Don S. Browning, M. Christian Green, and John Witte, Jr. (eds), *Sex, Marriage, and Family in World Religions* (New York: Columbia University Press, 2006).

13. The most notable collection on this topic remains Sarah Coakley (ed.), *Religion and the Body* (Cambridge: Cambridge University Press, 1997); also see Kimerer L. LaMothe, "What Bodies Know about Religion and the Study of It," *Journal of the American Academy of Religion* 76, no. 3 (September 2008): 573–601.

14. "Body," in *Critical Terms for Religious Studies*, ed. Mark C. Taylor (Chicago: University of Chicago Press, 1998), 38.

15. See Robert C. Fuller, *Spirituality in the Flesh: Bodily Sources of Religious Experience* (Oxford and New York: Oxford University Press, 2008).

16. See Miguel A. De La Torre, "Why a Journal Like This?," *Journal of Race, Ethnicity, and Religion* 1, no. 1 (2010): 1–11.

17. Craig R. Prentiss (ed.), *Religion and the Creation of Race and Ethnicity: An Introduction* (New York: New York University Press, 2003), 2.

18. For a succinct account of the most prominent theories of globalization, see Lionel Obadia, *Globalization and the Study of Religion*, in *The New Blackwell Companion to the Sociology of Religion*, ed. Bryan S. Turner (Malden, MA and Oxford: Blackwell Publishing, 2010), 477–83.

19. Bryan S. Turner, "Theories of Globalization: Issues and Origins," in *The Routledge International Handbook of Globalization Studies*, ed. Bryan S. Turner (New York: Routledge, 2010), 4.

20. To explore these issues further, see Peter Beyer and Lori Beaman (eds), *Religion, Globalization, and Culture* (Leiden: Brill, 2007); Derrick M. Nault, Bei Dawei, Evangelos Volgarakis, Rab Paterson, and Cesar Andres-Miguel Suva (eds), *Experiencing Globalization: Religion in Contemporary Contexts* (London and New York: Anthem Press, 2014).

21. "Thinking Globally about Religion," in *The Oxford Handbook of Global Religions*, ed. Mark Juergensmeyer (New York: Oxford University Press, 2006), 4.

22. *Crossing and Dwelling: A Theory of Religion* by Thomas Tweed (Cambridge, MA: Harvard University Press, 2006) is particularly sensitive to questions of identity and mobility in a globalized world.

23. For treatments of religion, diaspora, and the immigrant experience, see R. Stephen Warner and Judith G. Wittner (eds), *Gatherings in Diaspora: Religious Communities and the New Immigration* (Philadelphia, PA: Temple University Press, 1998); Diana L. Eck, *A New Religious America: How a*

"Christian Country" Has Become the World's Most Religiously Diverse Nation (New York: HarperCollins, 2001); and Juergensmeyer, "Thinking Globally about Religion," *The Oxford Handbook of Global Religions*, 5–8.

24. For additional reading on this topic, see James R. Lewis (ed.), *The Oxford Handbook of New Religious Movements* (Oxford and New York: Oxford University Press, 2004); Lorne L. Dawson, *Comprehending Cults: The Sociology of New Religious Movements*, 2nd ed. (New York: Oxford University Press, 2006); Olav Hammer and Mikael Rothstein (eds), *The Cambridge Companion to New Religious Movements* (Cambridge and New York: Cambridge University Press, 2012); and George D. Chryssides and Benjamin E. Zeller (eds), *The Bloomsbury Companion to New Religious Movements* (London and New York: 2014). For a discussion of the distinction between "cult" and "new religious movement," see J. Gordon Melton, "Introduction to New Religions," in *The Oxford Handbook of New Religious Movements*, 17–21.

25. Susan J. Palmer, "Caught Up in the Cult Wars: Confessions of a New Religious Movement Researcher" (http://blog.longreads.com/2013/09/28/caught-up-in-the-cult-wars-confessions-of-a-new/).

26. Susan J. Palmer, "Caught Up in the Cult Wars."

27. Scholars have shown that "New Age" has a clearly identifiable history, in contrast with the broader category, "spiritual," or "New Religious Movements." See Daren Kemp and James R. Lewis (eds), *Handbook of New Age* (Leiden: Brill, 2007); Steven J. Sutcliffe and Ingvild Sælid Gilhus (eds), *New Age Spirituality: Rethinking Religion* (London and New York: Routledge, 2014); and Roger E. Olson, "Whatever Happened to the New Age Movement (NAM)," *Patheos*, January 13, 2014 (http://www.patheos.com/blogs/rogereolson/2014/01/whatever-happened-to-the-new-age-movement-nam).

28. Kieran Flanagan, Introduction to *Sociology of Spirituality*, ed. Kieran Flanagan and Peter C. Jupp (Aldershot: Ashgate, 2007), 11.

29. In an important article, Nancy Ammerman in fact questions the prevalence of the "spiritual, not religious" identity itself; see "Spiritual But Not Religious? Beyond Binary Choices in the Study of Religion," *Journal for the Scientific Study of Religion* 52, no. 2 (2013): 258–78.

30. The term "fundamentalism" was originally used by American Protestants in the early twentieth century, leading some scholars to wonder whether it actually applies properly to other cases. See Henry Munson, "Fundamentalism," in *The Routledge Companion to the Study of Religion*, ed. John R. Hinnells (New York: Routledge, 2005), 342.

31. See Gabriel A. Almond, Emmanuel Sivan, and R. Scott Appleby, "Fundamentalism: Genus and Species," in *Fundamentalisms Comprehended*, ed. Martin E. Marty and R. Scott Appleby (Chicago: University of Chicago Press, 2005), 402–08.

32. For further analysis of this topic, see Karen Armstrong, *The Battle for God* (New York: Ballantine, 2000); Gabriel A. Almond, R. Scott Appleby and Emmanuel Silvan (eds), *Strong Religion: The Rise of Fundamentalisms around the World* (Chicago and London: The University of Chicago Press, 2003); the five volumes produced by *The Fundamentalism Project*, ed. Martin Marty and R. Scott Appleby (University of Chicago); Malise Ruthven, *Fundamentalism: A Very Short Introduction* (Oxford and New York: Oxford University Press, 2007).

33. Roger S. Gottlieb, "Introduction," *Liberating Faith: Religious Voices for Justice, Peace, and Ecological Wisdom*, ed. Roger S. Gottlieb (Lanham, MD: Rowman & Littlefield, 2003), xxviii.

34. Also see Leigh E. Schmidt and Sally M. Promey (eds), *American Religious Liberalism* (Bloomington: Indiana University Press, 2012).

35. Mark Washofsky, *Jewish Living: A Guide to Contemporary Reform Practice*, 2nd ed. (New York: UAHC Press, 2010), xvii–xix.

36. For a rich account of this remarkable event, see Melissa J. Wilde, *A Sociological Analysis of Religious Change* (Princeton, NJ: Princeton University Press, 2007).

37. Again, see Mark Juergensmeyer, *Terror and the Mind of God: The Global Rise of Religious Violence*, 3rd ed. (Berkeley: University of California Press, 2003). Also see Bryan Rennie and Philip L. Tite (eds), *Religion, Terror and Violence: Religious Studies Perspectives* (New York and London: Routledge, 2008); Ariel Glucklich, *Dying for Heaven: Holy Pleasure and Suicide Bombers— Why the Best Qualities of Religion Are Also Its Most Dangerous* (New York: HarperOne, 2009); Mark Juergensmeyer, Margo Kitts, and Michael Jerryson (eds), *The Oxford Handbook of Religion and Violence* (Oxford and New York: Oxford University Press, 2013); and Karen Armstrong, *Fields of Blood: Religion and the History of Violence* (New York: Alfred A. Knopf, 2014).

38. A number of popular books supporting this perspective have appeared in the last recent years, including Sam Harris, *The End of Faith: Religion, Terror, and the Future of Reason* (New York and London: W. W. Norton, 2005) and Christopher Hitchens, *God Is Not Great: How Religion Poisons Everything* (New York: Hachette Book Group, 2007).

39. Gerrie Ter Haar, "Religion: Source of Conflict or Resource for Peace?" in *Bridge or Barrier: Religion, Violence, and Visions for Peace*, ed. Gerrie ter Haar and James J. Busuttil (Leiden: Brill, 2005), 8.

40. John D. Carlson, "Religion and Violence: Coming to Terms with Terms," in *The Blackwell Companion to Religion and Violence*, ed. Andrew R. Murphy (West Sussex: Blackwell, 2011), 11.

41. William T. Cavanaugh, "The Myth of Religious Violence," in *The Blackwell Companion to Religion and Violence*, 32.

42. See Roger S. Gottlieb (ed.), *Liberating Faith*, for a volume dedicated to this theme.

43. See Richard Dawkins, *The God Delusion* (Boston, MA: Houghton Mifflin, 2006) and Daniel Dennett, *Breaking the Spell: Religion as a Natural Phenomenon* (New York: Viking, 2006).

44. Ian Barbour, *When Science Meets Religion: Enemies, Strangers, or Partners* (New York: HarperCollins, 2000), 2–4 and fl. Also see Barbour's *Religion and Science: Historical and Contemporary Issues*, rev. ed. (London: SCM Press, 1998), upon which *When Science Meets Religion* is based; Alister E. McGrath, *Science and Religion: A New Introduction*, 2nd ed. (Chcichester: Wiley-Blackwell, 2010); Brendan Sweetman, *Religion and Science: An Introduction* (London and New York: Continuum, 2010); and Philip Clayton, *Religion and Science: The Basics* (New York: Routledge, 2012).

45. Although it should be noted that scientists hold these beliefs at a significantly lower rate than the general populace (in the United States). "Scientists and Belief," November 5, 2009, Pew Research Center: Religion and Public Life (http://www.pewforum.org/2009/11/05/scientists-and-belief).

46. The Creation Museum in Petersburg, Kentucky. See http://creationmuseum. org. For an analysis of this site that draws upon theoretical perspectives in the academic study of religion, see Kelly E. Hayes, "Creationism and Evolution Are Competing 'Myths,'" *Religion Dispatches*, June 3, 2011 (http://religiondispatches.org/creationism-and-evolution-are-competing-myths).

47. According to Gallup polling In 2014, 42 percent of Americans subscribe to the view that "God created man pretty much in his present form at one time within the last 10,000 years or so" (http://www.religioustolerance.org/ev_publia.htm).

48. Léon Turner, "Introduction: Pluralism and Complexity in the Evolutionary Cognitive Science of Religion," in *Evolution, Religion, and Cognitive Science: Critical and Constructive Essays*, ed. Fraser Watts and Léon Turner (Oxford: Oxford University Press, 2014), 2. Touchstones in this area include Pascale Boyer, *Religion Explained: The Evolutionary Origins of Religious Thought* (New York: Basic Books, 2001); David Sloan Wilson, *Darwin's Cathedral: Evolution, Religion, and the Nature of Society* (Chicago: University of

Chicago Press, 2002); Daniel Dennett, *Breaking the Spell: Religion as a Natural Phenomenon* (New York: Penguin Books, 2006); and Robert C. Fuller, *Spirituality in the Flesh: Bodily Sources of Religious Experience*. See the website, "Evolutionary Religious Studies" (evolution.binghamton. edu/religion) for an excellent collection of resources and description of the contours of this emerging subfield.

49. Gary B. Ferngren, *Medicine and Religion: A Historical Introduction* (Baltimore, MD: Johns Hopkins University Press, 2014), 4–6.

50. For an extensive collection of resources on religions and their understanding of nature and the environment, see The Forum on Religion and Ecology at Yale website (fore.yale.edu).

51. For further reading, see Roger S. Gottlieb (ed.), *The Oxford Handbook of Religion and Ecology* (Oxford and New York: Oxford University Press, 2006); Whitney A. Bauman, Richard R. Bohannon II, and Kevin J. O'Brien (eds), *Grounding Religion: A Field Guide to the Study of Religion and Ecology* (Abingdon and New York: Routledge, 2011); and John Grim and Mary Evelyn Tucker, *Ecology and Religion* (Washington, DC: Island Press, 2014).

52. See David Morgan, "The Look of the Sacred," in *The Cambridge Companion to Religious Studies*, ed. Robert Orsi (New York: Cambridge University Press, 2012), 305.

53. Richard M. Carp, "Material Culture," in *The Routledge Handbook of Research Methods in the Study of Religion*, ed. Michael Stausberg and Steven Engler (Abingdon and New York: Routledge, 2011), 476.

54. "Material Religion," in *The Cambridge Companion to Religious Studies*, ed. Robert Orsi (New York: Cambridge University Press, 2012), 209.

55. For some background on this curious combination of theological profundity and seemingly random objects (and animals), see Corrie Mitchell, "Jesus, Bunnies, and Colored Eggs: An Explanation of Holy Week and Easter," April 15, 2014 (www.faithstreet.com/onfaith/2014/04/15/jesus-bunnies-and-colored-eggs-what-is-easter/31691).

56. For a superb meditation on the relationship between the religious and material culture, see S. Brent Plate, *A History of Religion in 5½ Objects: Bringing the Spiritual to Its Senses* (Boston, MA: Beacon Press, 2014). Plate's book focuses on stones, incense, drums, crosses, and bread.

57. For contemporary studies of religion and the arts, see David Morgan, *The Sacred Gaze: Religious Visual Culture in Theory and Practice* (Berkeley, Los Angeles, and London: University of California Press, 2005); S. Brent Plate (ed.), *Religion, Art, and Visual Culture: A Cross-Cultural Reader* (New York and Hampshire: Palgrave, 2002); and Frank Burch Brown (ed.), *The Oxford*

Handbook of Religion and the Arts (Oxford and London: Oxford University Press, 2014).

58. For an overview of this area of research, see Daniel A. Stout, Media and Religion: Foundations of an Emerging Field (Abingdon and New York: Routledge, 2012).

59. See, for example, Bruce David Forbes and Jeffrey H. Mahan (eds), Religion and Popular Culture in America, rev. ed. (Berkeley, Los Angeles, and London: University of California Press, 2005); Terry Ray Clark and Dan W. Clanton, Jr. (eds), Understanding Religion and Popular Culture (Abingdon and New York: Routledge, 2012); John C. Lyden and Eric Michael Mazur (eds), The Routledge Companion to Religion and Popular Culture (Abingdon and New York: Routledge, 2015); and the content of the Journal of Religion and Popular Culture (Toronto: University of Toronto Press).

60. See www.shyamji.com/pooja.html and www.scrapu.com/2008/09/online-virtual-puja.html, among many others.

61. For additional reading on this topic, see Lorne L. Dawson and Douglas E. Cowan (eds), Religion Online: Finding Faith on the Internet (London and New York: Routledge, 2004); Heidi A. Campbell (ed.), Digital Religion: Understanding Religious Practices in New Media Worlds (Abingdon and New York: Routledge, 2013).

62. William James, The Varieties of Religious Experience: A Study in Human Nature (New York: Penguin Books, 1982), 35.

# 6  Conclusion: Talking about Religion

In the summer of 2013, author Reza Aslan published a book called *Zealot: The Life and Times of Jesus of Nazareth*. As the title suggests, the work is an exploration of the historical identity of Jesus Christ. Aslan's thesis is provocative. According to him, Jesus was in his heart of hearts a political figure bent on rooting out corruption among his own people and ousting the Romans from his homeland. He was therefore a "zealot" for his cause, which was both religious and political, and that's what got him killed.

A provocative thesis, but not a terribly original one: Bible scholars have debated this idea for decades. Nevertheless, Aslan's book—and Aslan himself—made a media splash as the result of an interview he did with Lauren Green of Fox News right after the book came out. Green's opening question, which signaled the theme of the entire interview, was a bit surprising: "You are a Muslim, so why did you write a book about the founder of Christianity?" Aslan was somewhat taken aback. He answered, "Well, to be clear, I am a scholar of religions . . . who has been studying the origins of Christianity for decades, who also just happens to be a Muslim. So it's not that I'm just some Muslim writing about Jesus. I am an expert with a PhD in the history of religions," Green persisted with this line of questioning: "But it still begs the question [*sic*]: Why would you be interested in the founder of Christianity?" Aslan answered, "Because it's my job as an academic."

The exchange continued in this fashion, rather awkwardly gravitating around whether Aslan was qualified to write this book, because of his Muslim identity. While Green and Fox were roundly criticized for this rather derogatory approach, Aslan himself was also a bit awkward and defensive: he brandished (and slightly exaggerated) his academic qualifications to fend off the unexpected challenge. And was it *really* unexpected? Aslan has positioned himself in the past as a spokesman for Islam in America, so he is not unfamiliar with media exchanges like this, and he knows that they only enhance his public profile. As a result of the buzz created by his Fox interview, *Zealot* displaced J. K. Rowling's book, *The Casual Vacancy*, at the top of the *New York Times* bestsellers list.

And yet in the midst of this public relations/news-as-entertainment drama, important issues were at stake—issues that are relevant for you, as a student of religion. The fact is, *it is often difficult to talk about religion, and talking about what we do when we study it can be even more challenging.* In this instance, Aslan seemingly wanted to speak about his subject in one way, but his interviewer refused, insisting on another. Aslan claimed to be studying religion as an objective, academic, outside observer. His interviewer did not accept that. She attempted to undercut his authority and diminish his perspective, based on her perception of his identity.

As this book has often suggested, the position of a student or scholar of religion is a tricky one. Hopefully you are convinced about the importance of knowing about whatever it is that this term "religion" names, because it is directly relevant to being a global citizen and reflective human being. And despite the fact that the "how" of this branch of study is a matter of continuous debate and discussion, you now get the importance of developing theoretical literacy and joining in these conversations. But as secure as you might be in this mission, the Aslan case reminds us that difficulties and misperceptions persist. It *is* difficult to talk about religion—and not just for best-selling authors on cable news.

For example, let's imagine a hypothetical undergraduate who is on a two-and-a-half-hour flight, headed home for break. A stranger sits down in the seat next to her and decides to engage in conversation, to make the time pass. After the usual pleasantries, it is revealed that she is in college. And thus it begins:

"So, what are you majoring in?"

"Religion."

Now what? In many cases, because it is difficult to talk about this topic, the conversation ends there. The stranger says, "Oh," and the subject briefly changes, and then everyone retreats back into silence.

But it doesn't always go that way. If we imagine a more inquisitive seatmate, a whole line of questions emerges:

"Hmm. That's interesting. What are you going to do with that? Become a priest?"

Now our hypothetical student must do some thinking. How to answer?

"Well, it's an academic major, not training for a religious profession. So I'm not preparing to join the church or lead a congregation. I just want to understand religion and what makes religious people tick. And as to what to do with the major, I'm not exactly sure at this point. I guess I can do whatever I want. Maybe go to graduate school? Go to law school? Go out and get a job? Not sure."

The student is pointing out something that you know well by this point: the field is not reserved for the religious, or the nonreligious, for that matter. And unless you are in fact attending a specialized school that is religiously affiliated, its purpose is not to transform you into a more devout or pious follower. The academic study of religion promotes broad intellectual mastery, both in the widespread facts of religious phenomena and in the craft of analyzing and interpreting them. Its aim is not pre-professional or doctrinal training.

There is another issue at work behind this generally well-meaning question. Shouldn't your major—or even any individual course—help to translate into a job or a career? Here we touch upon a much bigger discussion about higher education that goes beyond the scope of this book. But we can note that parents and politicians these days are demanding that colleges and universities, which have become so expensive, recommit themselves to turning out graduates who can find jobs and get a return on their educational investment. Religious Studies, like many other majors that we have come to value, like Art History, Classics, Comparative Literature, English, History, Philosophy, and Sociology, among others, may not have an obvious professional application. It's difficult to find a lucrative entry-level position at a Fortune 500 company as a "Religion Expert."

So where does the academic study of religion fit into this wider debate? Is it practical as a course of study, or a mere indulgence—especially if you are not planning to be a guru, imam, monk, priest, nun, pastor, rabbi, or spiritual advisor? And here is the answer (and maybe something like this is on our hypothetical student's mind as she answers her travel companion): this field is just as practical as any major that provides the skills that are most in demand by both graduate schools and employers—if not more so. These include oral and written expression, the ability to

understand and analyze complex information, the capacity for empa-
thizing with and understanding alternative viewpoints, and simply put,
thinking outside the box.

So perhaps the best answer to the question, "What can you do with a
major in religious studies?" is—"What can't you do?"

Let's assume we make it past this stage of the hypothetical conversation. Where to from here?

"Well, that's great. Sounds like you might have a chance at a good
career. So . . . what religion are you?"

It is perhaps understandable that someone would want to know about
your own affiliation, when you tell him or her what you're studying. But this
next step in the conversation recalls the line of questioning that greeted
Aslan in his Fox News interview. Unfortunately it implies that the most
important reason one would study this material is because one is religious
oneself. Here our student has to outline the difference between one's
background and the academic enterprise.

"Well, I'm happy to tell you, but I have to say that it doesn't have that
much to do with my major. I am [Christian/Jewish/Muslim/Buddhist/
Hindu/Wiccan/atheist/agnostic/etc.], but that's separate from what I
study. I was trained to step back from my own background, and also
to be aware of my potential biases. Sometimes I still compare my
own background with what I'm studying; that can be helpful, but I try
not to let it get in the way."

We have discovered that in order to understand and effectively interpret
this content, it is important to be self-conscious, to maintain some distance,
and to manage our preconceived notions and agendas. There are many
different variations on and divergences from these basic principles. The
phenomenologist or social scientist insists that proper study requires objectivity and neutrality. Critics suggest that it is impossible to be completely
objective, that "bracketing" just doesn't work; we always involve our background and previous ideas in the process of understanding. Maybe claiming
the intellectual high ground, lording over our material under the pretense of
objectivity is even ethically problematic, for power (our power to observe)
and knowledge (what we choose to see) are intimately connected.

As our student seems to understand, these are tough debates, but
she presents a very reasonable response: in the end, she is not pushing

her own agenda, and she is not primarily motivated by a personal spiritual quest. As we have said before, this field is not designed to make you more religious or less religious; it promotes literacy and understanding within a refined analytical framework. Yes, it promotes self-knowledge, but this kind of knowledge is relevant to everyone, all global citizens, regardless of their tradition and heritage.

And so the dialogue continues.

"Wow. It's impressive that you can be so even-handed, but you must have some kind of opinion, based on everything that you have learned. Is religion in general a good thing or a bad thing? Or are some religions better than others? Which one is right?"

Now our student is facing an even bigger challenge: explaining the relationship between *normative* judgments (i.e., whether religion/a religious tradition is right or wrong, good or bad) and what she does in religious studies. We know that in general, while the discipline has received considerable energy and motivation from thinkers who wanted either to criticize or celebrate their subject, in its contemporary form, it is not generally geared toward making qualitative judgments. Instead, it encourages understanding and insight: we want to accurately describe, carefully analyze, productively compare, and properly explain religious phenomena—not judge them.

But maybe our student's fellow passenger has a point here. Why study this stuff, if we aren't ultimately interested in discovering the truth about it? However, we should note that there are different layers of truth. The student discovers the truth about the religion in a targeted manner: she gains a better sense of it, correcting misapprehensions and cultivating literacy. This is a simple but still challenging matter of *getting things right*. Here's an example. In the wake of 9/11, it was all too common for men with beards and turbans to be harassed and even attacked because they were thought to belong to the people who perpetrated the terrorist attack. One big problem (among many): these men were *Sikhs* and not Muslims. The truth is—the basic kind of truth that the religion student possesses—is that these are different traditions, with different histories, rituals, texts, and so on.

As we have discovered, however, the truth in this discipline does go deeper. Theories hopefully permit a kind of "deep seeing" that goes beyond the facts, revealing the nature of a community or individual's way of being—what they're *really* up to. And this is indeed where things get very tricky for our student: a statement about what religion *really* is about will almost inevitably have a *normative* content. If religion is really illusion, or opium, or an evolutionary vestige that is no longer necessary, then it is probably bad for us or wrong; if it answers our questions about the ultimate nature of things, connects us with what is "really real," or immerses us in personal or collective meaning, then it seems to be right and good. So, in this enterprise, have we at first avoided judgment just to come back to it?

There is a discipline, philosophy of religion, that is indeed committed to the project of developing reliable normative judgments about its subject matter. Up to this point, philosophers of religion (and one might say philosophers in general) have been relatively quick in their judgments, and devoted primarily (and one might say obsessed) with the claims of Christianity.[1] But the emergence of religious studies as an academic discipline has led to a new and welcome imperative: to judge religion, you have to understand it, and certainly not only one version of it. The pursuit of truth—whether something is ultimately good or bad; whether one tradition is right and the others wrong—may be unavoidable, and when it is embraced by reasonable, informed people, it is even noble. But the path to these answers now goes through the academic study of religion. Any normative conclusion that is not built on comparative, methodical, theoretically informed analysis should be deemed invalid.

So . . . this is not easy. How should our student respond?

"The thing is, I am not really in a position to answer those questions . . . I just want to know and understand how people live. To place one tradition above the others, or to say that religion as a whole is good or bad, that's not something that I am ready to answer. I think that if I keep at it, maybe I'll gain some insight on that question. Or, maybe, just maybe, my job is simply to be smart and informed about religion, and pass what I know on to others, so they can make better judgments for themselves. And doing that job well wouldn't be a bad thing at all."

Our student is doing her best with this very tough question, and maybe she is thinking about her mentors in formulating her response. Most religious studies scholars—just like scholars in so many other fields—have committed themselves to an interesting position: submerging themselves in a "bracketed" realm that hopefully provides a higher order of understanding—perhaps one that is ultimately on the way to the discovery of *THE* truth, but more likely, it remains in the service of others' discovery, one beginning student at a time.

So after all this, what else does our fellow passenger have to say? The flight is almost over; the time has passed; and we're almost done. But then it comes, the most inevitable and common response:

"Let me tell you *my* story . . . "

And now our student of religion is ready to listen.

## Note

1. See Timothy David Knepper, *The Ends of Philosophy of Religion: Terminus and Telos* (New York: Palgrave MacMillan, 2013) and Kevin Schilbrack, *Philosophy and the Study of Religions: A Manifesto* (Chichester: Wiley Blackwell, 2014).

# Additional Reading

The following list of resources invites you to continue your examination of religion. It contains general reference works, classic and contemporary texts in theory and method, and accessible treatments of a wide range of traditions, including Buddhism, Chinese Religions, Christianity, Indigenous and Ancient Religions, Islam, Japanese Religions, Judaism, Religion in America, and South Asian Religions. This list is necessarily partial and selective, but it provides a good starting point for further study and reflection.

## General Reference

Bowker, John. *World Religions: The Great Faiths Explored and Explained*. New York: DK, 2006.

Eliade, Mircea. *The Encyclopedia of Religion*. 2nd ed. Woodbridge, CT: Macmillan Reference, 2004.

Esposito, John L., Darrell J. Fasching, and Todd Lewis. *World Religions Today*. 5th ed. New York: Oxford University Press, 2005.

Hinnells, John R. *The Penguin Dictionary of Religions*. New York: Penguin Books, 1997.

Levinson, David. *Religion: A Cross-Cultural Dictionary*. New York: Oxford University Press, 1998.

Prothero, Stephen. *God Is Not One: The Eight Rival Religions That Run the World*. New York: HarperOne, 2010.

Sharma, Arvind. *Our Religions: The Seven World Religions Introduced by Preeminent Scholars from Each Tradition*. New York: HarperSanFrancisco, 1994.

Smart, Ninian. *The World's Religions*. 2nd ed. Cambridge: Cambridge University Press, 1998.

Smith, Huston. *The World's Religions: Our Great Wisdom Traditions*. Rev. ed. New York: HarperOne, 1991.

Smith, Jonathan Z., ed. *The HarperCollins Dictionary of Religion*. New York: HarperSanFrancisco, 1995.

# Approaches: Classic and Contemporary

Almond, Gabriel A., R. Scott Appleby, and Emmanuel Silvan, eds. *Strong Religion: The Rise of Fundamentalisms around the World*. Chicago and London: The University of Chicago Press, 2003.

Armstrong, Karen. *The Battle for God*. New York: Ballantine, 2000.

Armstrong, Karen. *Fields of Blood: Religion and the History of Violence*. New York: Alfred A. Knopf, 2014.

Barbour, Ian. *Religion and Science: Historical and Contemporary Issues*. Rev. ed. London: SCM Press, 1998.

Bauman, Whitney A., Richard R. Bohannon II, and Kevin J. O'Brien, eds. *Grounding Religion: A Field Guide to the Study of Religion and Ecology*. Abingdon and New York: Routledge, 2011.

Berger, Peter L. *The Sacred Canopy: Elements of a Sociological Theory of Religion*. New York: Anchor Books, 1990.

Boyer, Pascale. *Religion Explained: The Evolutionary Origins of Religious Thought*. New York: Basic Books, 2001.

Brown, Frank Burch, ed. *The Oxford Handbook of Religion and the Arts*. Oxford and London: Oxford University Press, 2014.

Browning, Don S., M. Christian Green, and John Witte, Jr., eds. *Sex, Marriage, and Family in World Religions*. New York: Columbia University Press, 2006.

Campbell, Heidi A., ed. *Digital Religion: Understanding Religious Practices in New Media Worlds*. Abingdon and New York: Routledge, 2013.

Campbell, Joseph and Bill Moyers. *The Power of Myth*. New York: Anchor Books, 2011.

Capps, Walter H. *Religious Studies: The Making of a Discipline*. Minneapolis, MN: Augsburg Fortress, 1995.

Castelli, Elizabeth, ed. *Women, Gender, Religion: A Reader*. New York: Palgrave, 2001.

Christ, Carol and Judith Plaskow, eds. *Womanspirit Rising: A Feminist Reader in Religion*. New York: HarperSanFrancisco, 1992.

Chryssides, George D. and Benjamin E. Zeller, eds. *The Bloomsbury Companion to New Religious Movements*. London and New York, 2014.

Clark, Terry Ray and Dan W. Clanton, Jr., eds. *Understanding Religion and Popular Culture*. Abingdon and New York: Routledge, 2012.

Clayton, Philip. *Religion and Science: The Basics*. New York: Routledge, 2012.

Coakley, Sarah, ed. *Religion and the Body*. Cambridge: Cambridge University Press, 1997.

Comstock, Gary David and Susan E. Henking, eds. *Que(e)rying Religion: A Critical Anthology*. London and New York: Continuum, 1997.

Dawson, Lorne L. *Comprehending Cults: The Sociology of New Religious Movements*. 2nd ed. New York: Oxford University Press, 2006.

Dawson, Lorne L. and Douglas E. Cowan, eds. *Religion Online: Finding Faith on the Internet.* London and New York: Routledge, 2004.

Dennett, Daniel. *Breaking the Spell: Religion as a Natural Phenomenon.* New York: Viking Penguin, 2006.

Douglas, Mary. *Purity and Danger: An Analysis of the Concepts of Pollution and Taboo.* London and New York: Routledge, 2002.

Durkheim, Émile. *The Elementary Forms of Religious Life.* Trans. Carol Cosman. New York: Oxford University Press, 2001.

Eliade, Mircea. *Patterns in Comparative Religion.* Trans. Rosemary Sheed. Lincoln, NE: Bison Books, 1996.

Eliade, Mircea. *The Sacred and the Profane: The Nature of Religion.* Trans. Willard R. Trask. Orlando, FL: Harcourt, 1987.

Ferngren, Gary B. *Medicine and Religion: A Historical Introduction.* Baltimore, MD: Johns Hopkins University Press, 2014.

Fiorenza, Elisabeth Schüssler. *In Memory of Her: A Feminist Theological Reconstruction of Christian Origins.* New York: Crossroad, 1983.

Forbes, Bruce David and Jeffrey H. Mahan, eds. *Religion and Popular Culture in America.* Rev. ed. Berkeley, Los Angeles, and London: University of California Press, 2005.

Freud, Sigmund. *The Future of an Illusion.* New York: W. W. Norton, 1989.

Fulkerson, Mary McClintock. *Changing the Subject: Women's Discourses and Feminist Theology.* Minneapolis, MN: Fortress Press, 1994.

Fuller, Robert C. *Spirituality in the Flesh: Bodily Sources of Religious Experience.* Oxford and New York: Oxford University Press, 2008.

Geertz, Clifford. *The Interpretation of Cultures.* New York: Basic Books, 1973.

Glucklich, Ariel. *Dying for Heaven: Holy Pleasure and Suicide Bombers—Why the Best Qualities of Religion Are Also Its Most Dangerous.* New York: HarperOne, 2009.

Gottlieb, Roger S., ed. *The Oxford Handbook of Religion and Ecology.* Oxford and New York: Oxford University Press, 2006.

Grim, John and Mary Evelyn Tucker. *Ecology and Religion.* Washington, DC: Island Press, 2014.

Gross Gross, Rita M. *Feminism and Religion.* 2nd ed. Boston, MA: Beacon Press, 1996.

Hammer, Olav and Mikael Rothstein, eds. *The Cambridge Companion to New Religious Movements.* Cambridge and New York: Cambridge University Press, 2012.

Hinnells, John R. *The Routledge Companion to the Study of Religion.* London and New York: Routledge, 2005.

James, William. *Varieties of Religious Experience.* London and New York: Routledge, 2002.

Juergensmeyer, Mark, ed. *The Oxford Handbook of Global Religions*. New York: Oxford University Press, 2006.

Juergensmeyer, Mark. *Terror and the Mind of God: The Global Rise of Religious Violence*. 3rd ed. Berkeley: University of California Press, 2003.

Juergensmeyer, Mark, Margo Kitts, and Michael Jerryson, eds. *The Oxford Handbook of Religion and Violence*. Oxford and New York: Oxford University Press, 2013.

Jung, C. G. *Psychology and Religion*. New Haven, CT and London: Yale University Press, 1966.

Juschka, Darlene, ed. *Feminism in the Study of Religion: A Reader*. London and New York: Continuum, 2001.

Kemp, Daren and James R. Lewis, eds. *Handbook of New Age*. Leiden: Brill, 2007.

King, Richard. *Orientalism and Religion: Postcolonial theory, India and "The Mystic East."* London and New York: Routledge, 1999.

King, Ursula, ed. *Religion and Gender*. Oxford and Malden, MA: Blackwell, 1995.

Lewis, James R., ed. *The Oxford Handbook of New Religious Movements*. Oxford and New York: Oxford University Press, 2004.

Lyden, John C. and Eric Michael Mazur, eds. *The Routledge Companion to Religion and Popular Culture*. Abingdon and New York: Routledge, 2015.

Masuzawa, Tomoko. *The Invention of World Religions: Or, How European Universalism Was Preserved in the Language of Pluralism*. Chicago and London: The University of Chicago Press, 2005.

McCarthy Brown, Karen. *Mama Lola: A Vodou Priestess in Brooklyn*. Berkeley and Los Angeles, CA: University of California Press, 2011.

McGrath, Alister E. *Science and Religion: A New Introduction*. 2nd ed. Chichester: Wiley-Blackwell, 2010.

Morgan, David. *The Sacred Gaze: Religious Visual Culture in Theory and Practice*. Berkeley, Los Angeles, and London: University of California Press, 2005.

Orsi, Robert. *Between Heaven and Earth: The Religious Worlds People Make and the Scholars Who Study Them*. Princeton, NJ: Princeton University Press, 2005.

Orsi, Robert, ed. *The Cambridge Companion to Religious Studies*. New York: Cambridge University Press, 2012.

Otto, Rudolf. *The Idea of the Holy*. Translated by John W. Harvey. New York: Oxford University Press, 1958.

Pals, Daniel L. *Eight Theories of Religion*. 2nd ed. New York: Oxford University Press, 2006.

Plate, S. Brent. *A History of Religion in 5½ Objects: Bringing the Spiritual to Its Senses*. Boston, MA: Beacon Press, 2014.

Plate, S. Brent, ed. *Religion, Art, and Visual Culture: A Cross-Cultural Reader*. New York and Hampshire: Palgrave, 2002.

Prentiss, Craig R., ed. *Religion and the Creation of Race and Ethnicity: An Introduction*. New York: New York University Press, 2003.

Rennie, Bryan and Philip L. Tite, eds. *Religion, Terror and Violence: Religious Studies Perspectives*. New York and London: Routledge, 2008.

Sharma, Arvind, ed. *Today's Woman in World Religions*. Albany: State University of New York Press, 1994.

Smith, Huston. *Why Religion Matters: The Fate of the Human Spirit in an Age of Disbelief*. New York: HarperSanFrancisco, 2001.

Smith, Jonathan Z. *Imagining Religion: From Babylon to Jonestown*. Chicago and London: University of Chicago Press, 1982.

Smith, Jonathan Z. *Relating Religion: Essays in the Study of Religion*. Chicago: University of Chicago Press, 2004.

Smith, Wilfred Cantwell. *The Meaning and End of Religion*. Minneapolis, MN: Augsburg Fortress, 1991.

Stout, Daniel A. *Media and Religion: Foundations of an Emerging Field*. Abingdon and New York: Routledge, 2012.

Sutcliffe, Steven J. and Ingvild Sælid Gilhus, eds. *New Age Spirituality: Rethinking Religion*. London and New York: Routledge, 2014.

Sweetman, Brendan. *Religion and Science: An Introduction*. London and New York: Continuum, 2010.

Taylor, Mark C., ed. *Critical Terms for Religious Studies*. Chicago and London: The University of Chicago Press, 1998.

Tillich, Paul. *Dynamics of Faith*. London: HarperCollins, 2001.

Tillich, Paul. *Theology of Culture*. New York: Oxford University Press, 1964.

Turner, Victor. *The Ritual Process: Structure and Anti-Structure*. Piscataway, NJ: Aldine Transaction, 1995.

Tweed, Thomas A. *Crossing and Dwelling: A Theory of Religion*. Cambridge, MA: Harvard University Press, 2006.

Van Gennep, Arnold. *The Rites of Passage*. London: Routledge, 2004.

Watts, Fraser and Léon Turner, eds. *Evolution, Religion, and Cognitive Science: Critical and Constructive Essays*. Oxford: Oxford University Press, 2014.

Wilson, David Sloan. *Darwin's Cathedral: Evolution, Religion, and the Nature of Society*. Chicago: University of Chicago Press, 2002.

Weber, Max. *The Protestant Ethic and the Spirit of Capitalism*. Trans. Stephen Kalberg. Oxford: Blackwell, 2002.

## Buddhism

Eckel, Malcolm David. *Buddhism: Origins, Beliefs, Practices, Holy Texts, Sacred Places*. New York: Oxford University Press, 2002.

Gethin, Rupert. *The Foundations of Buddhism*. New York: Oxford University Press, 1998.

Harvey, Peter. *An Introduction to Buddhism: Teachings, History and Practices.* 2nd ed. Cambridge: Cambridge University Press, 2013.

Keown, Damien. *Buddhism: A Very Short Introduction.* 2nd ed. Oxford: Oxford University Press, 2013.

Lopez, Donald S. *The Story of Buddhism: A Concise Guide to Its History and Teachings.* New York: HarperCollins, 2001.

Paul, Diana Y. *Women in Buddhism: Images of the Feminine in the Mahayana Tradition.* 2nd ed. Berkeley: University of California Press, 1985.

Prebish, Charles and Damien Keown. *Introducing Buddhism.* New York and London: Routledge, 2010.

Rahula, Walpola. *What the Buddha Taught.* New York: Grove Press, 1974.

Robinson, Richard H., Willard L. Johnson, and Thanisarro Bhikkhu. *Buddhist Religions: A Historical Introduction.* 5th ed. Belmont, CA: Wadsworth, 2004.

Smith, Huston and Philip Novak. *Buddhism: A Concise Introduction.* San Francisco: HarperSanFrancisco, 2004.

## Chinese Religions (including Confucianism and Daoism)

Adler, Joseph A. *Chinese Religious Traditions.* New York: Pearson, 2002.

Ching, Julia. *Chinese Religions.* Maryknoll, NY: Orbis Books, 1993.

Gardner, Daniel K. *Confucianism: A Very Short Introduction.* Oxford and New York: Oxford University Press, 2014.

Kohn, Livia. *Introducing Daoism.* New York: Routledge, 2009.

Komjathy, Louis. *The Daoist Tradition: An Introduction.* London and New York: Bloomsbury, 2013.

Miller, James. *Daoism: A Short Introduction.* Oxford: Oneworld Publications, 2003.

Overmyer, Daniel L. *Religions of China: The World as a Living System.* Rev. ed. Long Grove, IL: Waveland Press, 1998.

Poceski, Mario. *Introducing Chinese Religions.* New York: Routledge, 2009.

Sun, Anna. *Confucianism as a World Religion: Contested Histories and Contemporary Realities.* Princeton, NJ: Princeton University Press, 2013.

Xinzhong Yao. *An Introduction to Confucianism.* Cambridge: Cambridge University Press, 2000.

Xinzhong Yao and Yanxia Zhao. *Chinese Religion: A Contextual Approach.* London and New York, 2010.

## Christianity

Barrett, David B., George Thomas Kurian, and Todd M. Johnson, eds. *World Christian Encyclopedia: A Comparative Survey of Churches and Religions in the Modern World.* 2nd ed. New York: Oxford University Press, 2001.

Brakke, David and Weaver, Mary Jo. *Introduction to Christianity*. 4th ed. Belmont, CA: Wadsworth, 2009.

Crossan, John D. *Jesus: A Revolutionary Biography*. New York: HarperOne, 2009.

Ehrman, Bart D. *How Jesus Became God: The Exaltation of a Jewish Preacher from Galilee*. New York: HarperOne, 2014.

Fredriksen, Paula. *From Jesus to Christ: The Origins of the New Testament Images of Christ*. 2nd ed. New Haven, CT: Yale University Press, 2008.

González, Justo L. *The Story of Christianity, Vol. 1: The Early Church to the Dawn of the Reformation*. 2nd ed. New York: HarperOne, 2010.

González, Justo L. *The Story of Christianity, Vol. 2: The Reformation to the Present Day*. 2nd ed. New York: HarperOne, 2010.

Lindberg, Carter, ed. *A Brief History of Christianity*. Malden, MA and Oxford: Blackwell, 2006.

McManners, John. *The Oxford Illustrated History of Christianity*. New York: Oxford University Press, 2001.

Pagels, Elaine. *The Gnostic Gospel*. New York: Vintage Books, 1989.

Sanders, E. P. *The Historical Figure of Jesus*. London: Penguin, 1996.

Ware, Timothy. *The Orthodox Church: An Introduction to Eastern Christianity*. Rev. ed. London: Penguin, 2015.

Woodhead, Linda. *Christianity: A Very Short Introduction*. New York: Oxford University Press, 2005.

# Indigenous and Ancient Religions

Bottero, Jean. *Religion in Ancient Mesopotamia*. Trans. Teresa Lavender Fagan. Chicago: University of Chicago Press, 2004.

Eliade, Mircea. *Shamanism*. Trans. Willard R. Trask. Princeton, NJ: Princeton University Press, 2004.

Evans-Pritchard, Edward. *Nuer Religion*. New York: Oxford University Press, 1971.

Gill, Sam. *Native American Religions: An Introduction*. 2nd ed. Belmont, CA: Wadsworth Publishing, 2004.

Hackett, Rosalind. *Art and Religion in Africa*. London: Cassell, 1999.

Lewis, I. M. *Ecstatic Religion*. 3rd ed. London: Routledge, 2003.

Magesa, Laurenti. *African Religion: The Moral Traditions of Abundant Life*. Maryknoll, NY: Orbis Books, 1997.

Martin, Joel W. *The Land Looks After Us: A History of Native American Religion*. New York: Oxford University Press, 2001.

Mbiti, John S. *Introduction to African Religion*. 2nd ed. Long Grove, IL: Waveland Press, 2015.

Myerhoff, Barbara G. *Peyote Hunt: The Sacred Journey of the Huichol Indians*. Ithaca, NY: Cornell University Press, 1976.

Olupona, Jacob K. *African Religions: A Very Short Introduction*. Oxford and New York: Oxford University Press, 2014.

Ray, Benjamin C. *African Religions: Symbol, Ritual, and Community*. 2nd ed. Belmont, CA: Prentice Hall, 1999.

Shafer, Byron E., John R. Baines, David Silverman, and Leonard H. Lesko. *Religion in Ancient Egypt: Gods, Mytsh, and Personal Practice*. Ithaca, NY: Cornell University Press, 1991.

Sullivan, Lawrence, ed. *Native Religions and Cultures of North America: Anthropology of the Sacred*. London: Continuum, 2003.

Swain, Tony and Garry Trompf. *The Religions of Oceania*. London and New York: Routledge, 1995.

Tripolitis, Antonia. *Religions of the Hellenistic-Roman Age*. Grand Rapids, MI: Wm. B. Eerdmans Publishing Company, 2001.

Turnbull, Colin. *The Forest People*. New York: Touchstone, 1961.

# Islam

Armstrong, Karen. *Muhammad: A Biography of the Prophet*. New York: HarperCollins, 1993.

Denny, Frederick. *An Introduction to Islam*. 4th ed. Belmont, CA: Prentice Hall, 2011.

Esposito, John L. *Islam: The Straight Path*. 4th ed. New York: Oxford University Press, 2011.

Esposito, John L. *What Everyone Needs to Know about Islam*. New York: Oxford University Press, 2002.

Haider, Najam. *Shi'i Islam: An Introduction*. New York: Cambridge University Press, 2014.

Nasr, Seyyed Hossein. *Islam: Religion, History, and Civilization*. New York: HarperSanFrancisco, 2002.

Ruthven, Malise. *Islam: A Very Short Introduction*. Rev. ed. New York: Oxford University Press, 2012.

Schimmel, Annemarie. *Mystical Dimensions of Islam*. Chapel Hill: University of North Carolina Press, 1978.

# Japanese Religions

Earhart, H. Byron. *Religion in the Japanese Experience: Sources and Interpretations*. 2nd ed. Belmont, CA: Wadsworth Publishing, 1997.

Ellwood, Robert S. *Introducing Japanese Religion*. New York: Routledge, 2008.

Ellwood, Robert S. and Richard Pilgrim. *Japanese Religion: A Cultural Perspective*. Belmont, CA: Prentice Hall, 1984.

Kasulis, Thomas P. *Shinto: The Way Home*. Honolulu: University of Hawaii Press, 2004.

Kitagawa, Joseph. *On Understanding Japanese Religion*. Princeton, NJ: Princeton University Press, 1987.

## Judaism

de Lange, Nicholas. *An Introduction to Judaism*. 2nd ed. Cambridge: Cambridge University Press, 2010.

Fishbane, Michael. *Judaism: Revelation and Traditions*. New York: HarperCollins, 1987.

Friedman, Richard E. *Who Wrote the Bible?* New York: HarperCollins, 1997.

Heschel, Abraham Joshua. *The Sabbath*. New York: Farrar, Straus and Giroux, 2005.

Holtz, Barry W. *Back to the Sources: Reading the Classic Jewish Texts*. New York: Simon and Schuster, 1986.

Neusner, Jacob. *Judaism: The Basics*. London and New York: Routledge, 2006.

Scholem, Gershom. *Major Trends in Jewish Mysticism*. New York: Schocken Books, 1995.

Solomon, Norman. *Judaism: A Very Short Introduction*. New York: Oxford University Press, 2000.

Wouk, Herman. *This Is My God*. Boston: Back Bay Books, 1988.

## Religion in America

Ahlstrom, Sydney E. *A Religious History of the American People*. 2nd ed. New Haven, CT: Yale University Press, 2004.

Albanese, Catherine L. *A Republic of Mind and Spirit: A Culture History of American Metaphysical Religion*. New Haven, CT: Yale University Press, 2008.

Cohen, Charles L. and Ronald L. Numbers, eds. *Gods in America: Religious Pluralism in the United States*. Oxford and New York: Oxford University Press, 2013.

Eck, Diana. *A New Religious America: How a "Christian Country" Has Become the World's Most Religiously Diverse Nation*. New York: HarperCollins, 2009.

Griffith, R. Marie. *American Religions: A Documentary History*. New York and Oxford: Oxford University Press, 2008.

Manseau, Peter. *One Nation, Under God: A New American History*. New York: Little, Brown and Company, 2015.

Melton, J. Gordon. *Encyclopedic Handbook of Cults in America*. London and New York: Routledge, 1992.

Prothero, Stephen. *American Jesus: How the Son of God Became a National Icon*. New York: Farrar, Straus and Giroux, 2003.

Tabor, James. D. and Eugene V. Gallagher. *Why Waco? Cults and the Battle for Religious Freedom in America*. Berkeley: University of California Press, 1997.

Tweed, Thomas A., ed. *Retelling U.S. Religious History*. Berkeley: University of California Press, 1997.

## South Asian religions (Hinduism, Sikhism, Jainism)

Dundas, Paul. *The Jains*. 2nd ed. London and New York: Routledge, 2002.

Eck, Diana. *Darsan: Seeing the Divine Image in India*. 3rd ed. New York: Columbia University Press, 1996.

Flood, Gavin. *An Introduction to Hinduism*. Cambridge: Cambridge University Press, 1996.

Huyler, Stephen. P. and Thomas Moore. *Meeting God: Elements of Hindu Devotion*. New Haven, CT: Yale University Press, 2002.

Knipe, David. *Hinduism: Experiments in the Sacred*. Long Grove, IL: Waveland Press, 1998.

Knott, Kim. *Hinduism: A Very Short Introduction*. New York: Oxford University Press, 2000.

Mann, Gurinder Singh. *Sikhism*. Upper Saddle River, NJ: Prentice Hall, 2003.

Nesbitt, Eleanor. *Sikhism: A Very Short Introduction*. Oxford and New York: Oxford University Press, 2005.

Rodrigues, Hillary. *Introducing Hinduism.* London and New York: Routledge, 2006.

# Index